DISCOVERING
THE POWER OF
SELF-HYPNOSIS

D1495513

Urge
Choice
Act

DISCOVERING THE POWER OF SELF-HYPNOSIS

A NEW APPROACH FOR ENABLING CHANGE AND PROMOTING HEALING

Stanley Fisher, Ph.D.

with James Ellison

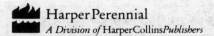

HarperPerennial
A Division of HarperCollinsPublishers

This book is available on tape from HarperAudio, a Division of HarperCollins Publishers.

PERMISSIONS

Excerpt from *Trance & Treatment: Clinical Uses of Hypnosis*, by Herbert Spiegel, M.D. and David Spiegel, M.D. Copyright © 1978 by Herbert Spiegel, M.D. and David Spiegel, M.D. Reprinted by permission of Basic Books, Inc., Publishers, New York.

Excerpt from *Clear Pictures* by Reynolds Price reprinted with the permission of Atheneum Publishers, an imprint of Macmillan Publishing Company, and the Harriet Wasserman Literary Agency. © 1989 by Reynolds Price.

DISCOVERING THE POWER OF SELF-HYPNOSIS: A NEW APPROACH FOR ENABLING CHANGE AND PROMOTING HEALING. Copyright © 1991 by Stanley Fisher, Ph.D. All rights reserved. Printed in the United States of America. No part of this book may be used or reproduced in any manner whatsoever without written permission except in the case of brief quotations embodied in critical articles and reviews. For information, address HarperCollins Publishers, Inc., 10 East 53rd Street, New York, NY 10022.

HarperCollins books may be purchased for educational, business, or sales promotional use. For information, please call or write: Special Markets Department, HarperCollins Publishers, Inc., 10 East 53rd Street, New York, NY 10022. Telephone: (212) 207-7528; Fax: (212) 207-7222.

First HarperPerennial edition published 1992.

LIBRARY OF CONGRESS CATALOG CARD NUMBER 90-55927
ISBN 0-06-092150-1

92 93 94 95 96 DT/HC 10 9 8 7 6 5 4 3 2 1

CONTENTS

To Joseph Barnett, M.D. (1926–1986) who guided a major part of my journey toward self-knowledge and made a difference in my life for which I am forever grateful.

ACKNOWLEDGMENTS

THIS BOOK would not have been possible without the assistance and support of these people with whom I share, and have shared, my professional life and pursuits: Dr. Herbert Spiegel, a teacher, clinician, and friend of rare ability and talent; Dr. Marcia Greenleaf, a caring and skillful clinician and my able colleague in research; the late Dr. Ralph Crowley, my first supervising analyst; Dr. Diana Greenwald, analyst and colleague, who inspired me to take the leap and move from research into clinical work; the faculty and fellow students of New York University's Post Doctoral Program in Psychoanalysis and Psychotherapy, for their insights, sharing and analytic training; Associate Dean, Dr. Jack Wilder and the department of Cardio-Thoracic Surgery at Albert Einstein College of Medicine in New York, for giving me the opportunity to conduct research exploring the use of hypnosis and surgery; and my extraordinary patients, a number of whom graciously lent their stories for adaptation in this book. In addition to expanding my understanding of human behavior and values, I thank them for showing me new definitions for forbearance, courage and optimism.

Also, there would be no book without my collaborator, the talented novelist and book editor, Jim Ellison, whose respect for language and good writing and for "hearing" my voice contributed immeasurably to make this book "mine." The thoughtful insights, reactions, and support of my adventurous editor at HarperCollins, Carol Cohen, were invaluable to us both.

A number of other friends and colleagues gave valuable time and advice along the way, among them: Howard Siegman, Keith Hollaman, Lori Horak, Elly Sidel, Sandy Stern, Kirk D'Amico, Joan Cunliffe, Donal Logue, and Maxine Marx.

Of course, my family holds a special place in my gratitude. Lillian and Sidney Rosen, my very dear sister and brother-in-law, were the first to introduce me, at age 19, to the concepts of psychotherapy and psychoanalysis; my sisters-in-law, Rhodie Margolis and Barbara Margolis, who provided early, very helpful feedback; my children and their spouses, Paul and Gloria Fisher, and Julia Fisher and Rafael Medina, and my grandchildren, Danny and Rachel Fisher, have never faltered in their love and devotion.

My wife, Esther Molly Margolis, with whom I share a very special love, was, without question, the major guiding force behind this book. An exceptional editor and publisher in her own right through her own company, Newmarket Press, she recognized the impact of my work before I did, and applied her considerable expertise to make a popular book happen that could reach a broad readership and make a difference in people's lives.

Stanley Fisher, Ph.D
December, 1990
New York City

INTRODUCTION

MOST PEOPLE decide to enter therapy because they want to eliminate a problem that is causing them pain and anxiety. They have come to understand that in order to function more fully, change is crucial and they are seeking to change their lives by learning to control and better understand their own feelings, reactions and behavior. Their search is for new and creative ways to move forward in life.

The 1970s brought a therapeutic revolution, and with it an acceptance of a variety of approaches to help individuals overcome their difficulties. Using methods ranging from physical manipulation, breathing, interpretation of dreams, visualization and role-playing, to self-hypnosis, biofeedback, relaxation, and meditation, we found we could teach the conscious mind to actively participate in inner journeys of discovery and self-empowerment. We began to realize that we could take our lives into our own hands—that we could teach ourselves how to breathe, how to eat, how to laugh, how to relieve pain, how to heal, how to eradicate bad habits, how to exercise, and how to relate to others in ways that would enhance and energize us. We could even change the body's internal functions, which were previously believed to be beyond the control of the individual. The power to change—physically and psychologically—is a power that lies within us, waiting to be tapped. What we lack is a comprehensive knowledge of how to tap into that power in ways that can work for each individual.

Over the past 12 years, I have used self-hypnosis as a technique to help more than 2,000 patients make changes in their lives. By combining self-hypnosis with my practice in psychoanalysis and short-term therapy, I have discovered how self-hypnosis can be used to provide structure and support when we choose to change our behavior or heighten our awareness. I have seen how knowledge of its principles and applications can return to each of us a power we were born with, but do not knowingly use. I have witnessed through my patients—and experienced for myself—how the regular use of a simple 90-second self-hypnosis exercise can help instruct our bodies and minds to alleviate such problems as insomnia, performance anxiety, fear of flying, depression, stress, overeating, memory loss, and smoking. I have marveled at the success of self-hypnosis in dealing with skin allergies, back pain, headaches, and kidney stones, and am especially impressed with its use as a preparation for surgery, which is one of my specialties. After much restless questioning and scientific skepticism, I came to see the strength of self-hypnosis as one of the techniques that can help most of us talk to—and be friends with—our bodies and minds.

In this book, I want to share with you the exploration, discovery and knowledge of hypnosis as an approach for therapy, diagnosis, and changing behavior and promoting healing. I hope that by passing on the sum of my personal and professional experience—by helping you redirect the hypnotic capacity you were born with but may not have used constructively since infancy—you will be empowered to live a better and fuller life, over which you will have a greater command than ever before.

Chapter *I*

DISCOVERING
THE POWER WITHIN:

The Myths vs. the Reality

MY JOURNEY of discovery began in 1977 when an associate of mine in the College of Physicians and Surgeons
at Columbia University in New York City sought hypnotic treatment to banish cigarettes from her life, and
I saw it work for her with relative ease. At the time, I
had only a passing knowledge of hypnosis. I had read
a few books in my twenties about how to put subjects
into a state of trance, had started taking classes, and
had experimented on friends and family members. I
found it a simple procedure to learn. I mastered it
quickly and felt amazingly powerful because of the
way in which good hypnotic subjects respond. But, I
also felt very uneasy and after I witnessed the misuse
of hypnosis by a stage hypnotist, I swore I wouldn't
practice it again without professional training. Over
the next several decades, my interest in hypnosis was
occasionally stimulated by something I read, but if I
hadn't decided to tackle a long time smoking problem

when I watched my associate conquer her habit, I might never have changed my professional focus from research to clinical psychology and become a psychoanalyst with a special involvement in hypnosis.

Like my associate at Columbia, I was also dependent on cigarettes. I was smoking close to 3 packs a day and my habit was 35 years old. Reasoning that if it worked for her, it could work for me, I called the person who had helped her, the psychiatrist Herbert Spiegel, for an appointment. Spiegel had been working with hypnosis since World War II and was one of the foremost people in the field. He had no appointment immediately available and, rather than wait, I accepted his referral to a colleague, psychiatrist Barbara DeBetz. DeBetz took me through a single 50-minute treatment session in which she evaluated my hypnotic capacity as mid-range, and taught me a self-hypnosis exercise to use in order to stop smoking. I used the exercise frequently for three weeks until I knew I had changed my habit. Without quite knowing it, I had entered a new, powerful dimension of myself by learning another way to change my behavior (I had already been through an analysis). My exploration of the power of self-hypnosis had begun.

That day in DeBetz's office, she suggested that I might benefit from attending the two courses Spiegel was giving at Columbia—Hypnosis in Medicine and Hypnosis in Psychiatry. My curiosity piqued, I cleared my schedule at the university and, that winter, participated in 10 full days of classes. I learned to evaluate an individual's hypnotic capacity, how to teach self-hypnosis, and how to use the patient's imagination and understanding to cope with problems.

I practiced the self-hypnosis technique over the

next few months on volunteer subjects and incorporated the use of self-hypnosis into a research proposal on pregnant women and smoking. I studied the literature in clinical and experimental hypnosis, and pursued post-doctoral training in psychoanalysis and psychotherapy. Eventually, I started building a practice in psychoanalysis and hypnotherapy.

Early in my practice, I saw the power of self-hypnosis in my work with patients—and particularly with my first surgical patient, Marcus, whose experience I describe in Chapter 2. It soon became clear to me that those who use self-hypnosis before undergoing surgery suffer less pain and anxiety and recover more quickly in the post operative phase than those who rely solely on sedation, muscle relaxants, and pain killers. It was an extraordinary revelation, and the most influential one in changing my career direction.

Alice, a patient who suffered terrible attacks of itching that immobilized her, gave me further validation of the power of self-hypnosis. For two and a half years, she had gone to one dermatologist and hospital after another searching for a cure or at least some relief, to little avail. Through my work with Alice (described in Chapter 5), I grasped the dramatic relationship between body and mind and was able to teach her to use self-hypnosis, her visceral memory, and her imagination to alleviate her incessant itching.

Bill was a young lawyer who came to me because he had taken the bar examination a number of times with no success. He knew the material and yet he couldn't pass. The minute Bill walked into the examination room his mind went blank; he could barely remember his name, let alone torts. Self-hypnosis helped him pass the exam, just as it helped another patient, Paul, to overcome a heavy 20-year smoking habit, and Martha to solve a life-long weight problem (the latter two cases are discussed in detail in Chapter 4). In case after case, both medical and psychological, patients helped me understand how to apply the technique of self-hypnosis. Patients and others showed me that self-hypnosis works when the patient follows a prescribed regimen, and psychological and medical problems, whether they be complex or simple, can often be alleviated without extensive treatment.

It still astonishes me how many people—new patients, friends, or acquaintances—are afraid of hypnosis, after all that has become known about it. I find that those people who are afraid usually lack personal experience with self-hypnosis. They imagine the stage hypnotist performing a kind of magic trick on subjects. Their response is, "Oh no, I'm not interested. I'm not going to let someone else play around with my mind." They think to themselves: "Maybe I'll be put under and something will go wrong." What they fear is loss of control. They see hypnosis as turning over power to another person.

By examining some of the myths surrounding hypnosis, it is possible to arrive at a better understanding of just what hypnosis is and what it is not.

Myth #1: During hypnosis, the subject is under the control of the hypnotist.

When we see a stage hypnotist at work in a nightclub or in a movie, it is easy to believe the myth is true. Although it seems as if the performer has some magical power, what he actually has is knowledge. Through personal instruction, observation, and books like *The Encyclopedia Of Stage Hypnotism* and *Techniques of*

Speed Hypnosis, the stage hypnotist is taught to "work" the audience before the performance; that is, he learns techniques for identifying volunteers with a high hypnotic capacity who will unconsciously fully support the performance. As long as subjects don't feel threatened, they will do what the stage hypnotist commands.

In reality, *all* hypnosis is *self*-hypnosis; the subject is always in control. Contrary to common belief, the subject is not under someone else's power, nor is he asleep. In fact, he is hyperalert and concentrating at a high level. In this mental state, he can have his experience structured by a therapist or hypnotist, but the choice of whether to cooperate or not is his alone.

Myth #2: There is no hypnosis without the hypnotist.

On the contrary, we often enter as well as leave trance states without being aware of it. Have you ever wondered what happened to those four hours while you were writing an important paper? Or where that two-hour stretch of time went while you were driving on the freeway? Have you ever sat at your desk so engrossed that you lost the awareness of things going on around you? Have you ever watched lovers walking down the street, arm in arm, so involved in each other the rest of the world does not exist for them? These are only a few examples among many of spontaneous trance experiences. Our lives are full of such examples of this normal, unbidden trance state.

Myth #3: Hypnosis is a form of sleep.

In the movies, one of the hypnotist's opening lines is "Your eyes are heavy and you're getting sleepy." Although the word hypnosis is derived from the Greek word for sleep, *hypnos*, hypnosis is, on the contrary, a relaxed state of focused concentration. In a study of the self-regulation of physiological processes, Jonathan Cohen, a psychologist, and Keith Sedlacek, a physician, reported that attention—obviously the opposite of sleep—is the underlying cognitive process common to most relaxation/self-regulation procedures. In trance, the patient is unusually aware and responsive and, unless told otherwise, tends to remember what went on during and after the experience. People under hypnosis whose eyes are closed may look like they're asleep, but their electroencephalogram (EEG) readings tell the true story: During hypnosis, there is a high incidence of alpha wave activity that indicates a relaxed yet attentive brain.

Myth #4: Female subjects and people with low IQ's are the most hypnotizable.

This commonly-held belief, popularized by movies and fiction, is pure make-believe. Research shows that hypnotizability is not gender-specific, and that, even though some intelligent people apparently have relatively little hypnotic capacity, keen concentration and focus are required to sustain an effective state of trance. (Writers of fiction and musicians, who are both creative and have vivid imaginations, are often the best hypnotic subjects.) Furthermore, research suggests that there is a reduced capacity for trance in patients with thought and affective disorders, as these patients usually find it difficult to maintain the required concentration.

The ability to be hypnotized is actually a capacity that can be measured through one of several evaluation procedures. (The procedure I use, the Hypnotic Induction Profile—the HIP—which is described in detail in Chapter 3, measures capacity on a scale of zero to four.) Studies indicate that most of the adult population is somewhat hypnotizable, and about 5–15 percent have a very high capacity. With the exception of those few people (about 5 percent) who are unable to respond, everyone, no matter what their range, can induce trance for constructive purposes.

Myth #5: Hypnosis has only recently begun to gain respectability in the scientific community.

In the early 1800s, hypnosis, although the subject of much dispute, was recognized as a powerful tool in healing, anesthesia, and self-improvement, and was slowly gaining acceptance by some factions of organized medicine. Hypnosis then faded out for more than 50 years, resurfacing briefly in the late nineteenth century with the work of Janet, Bernheim and Freud, and then again in the 1930s and 1940s, with the influential work of psychiatrist Milton H. Erickson. By the late 1950s, both the American Medical Association and the British Medical Society had approved the use of hypnosis as a valid therapeutic technique. Today, several national, professional societies of hypnosis are flourishing and more than 20,000 doctors, nurses, dentists, psychiatrists, social workers, and psychologists use hypnosis as a clinical technique, and that number is growing.

Myth #6: Hypnosis is therapeutic.

The hypnotic state is neither therapeutic nor nontherapeutic; it is a receptive environment or mental setting that can be used to explore the mind and to foster change. As Louis Alexander defined it in the *American Journal of Clinical Hypnosis*, hypnosis is "a state manifested by an inward turning of mind, facilitating an enhancement of the creative imagination, . . . and reducing the need for reality testing, thus providing a mental setting in which, with appropriate suggestions, ideas can be perceived and experienced in . . . a vivid manner."

Hypnosis sets up the communication between mind and body and, in that state of communication, you have the potential to use all of your understanding and ability, assuming you're provided with an entree —a strategy for effectively dealing with your problem. That is where the professional comes in. The professional serves as a teacher and a guide; someone who can help you learn to gain entree. However you are in command and you do the work yourself.

Myth #7: Hypnosis is mystical.

There is nothing mystical or magical about self-hypnosis. What is powerful (and therefore *seems* magical) is the access hypnosis provides to feelings, memories, and the systems of the body.

So, once we strip away the myths, what exactly is self-hypnosis? The hypnotic state itself—often called trance—can be described as a plateau of heightened awareness with external vigilance subdued, or as a relaxed state of focused concentration. For most of us, this state is a safe and comfortable place in which our conscious awareness of the external world fades away; a state in which we have an enhanced capacity for imagery and for communication with both body and mind.

When demonstrating the hypnotic state at work, Louis J. West, a physician, tells of a classic experiment:

"A cat lies in his cage listening to a clock going tick tick tick, and every time that the tick comes, a little electrode in the cat's head goes blip blip blip, and then a mouse is presented. The cat concentrates his attention on the mouse. The ticks continue but the blips disappear. Now, where have they gone? Why has the cat stopped hearing the ticks?"

The cat has entered a hypnotic state of heightened awareness; its external vigilance has been subdued. The clock is still ticking, but the cat no longer hears it or reacts to it. Its focus is elsewhere. This rapid entry into focused concentration is what the hypnotic experience is all about.

We can consciously and voluntarily invoke this mental setting—this state of heightened awareness—and that's where the technique of self-hypnosis comes in. I like to think of it as a pathway to a very special place: a room within ourselves. Once in the room, we can experience suggestions and ideas in a vivid manner; we are relaxed and open. Within this room—this state of focused concentration and inner communication—we can create and employ a strategy to restructure our thoughts, beliefs, feelings and responses. Psychiatrist Milton Erickson argues that even in hypnosis, the results of suggestion derive not from the therapist but from the life experiences of the patient. "Hypnosis," he explains, "does not change people nor does it alter their past experiential life. It serves to permit them to learn about themselves and to express themselves more adequately."

Through self-hypnosis, we have a means of stepping forward in our lives—for reaching our optimum potential. For example, a friend of my wife's and mine learned self-hypnosis to help her through an emergency hysterectomy. She had been bleeding for a number of days and was in poor shape. I arranged to see her at the hospital and taught her a self-hypnosis exercise she could use while the nurse was drawing blood—a common procedure, but one that was causing her a great deal of trouble. I also taught her a second exercise to use for surgery as well as postoperatively. She was operated on the next day and made an excellent recovery. At a dinner some months later, our friend asked me if she could adapt the technique to control her weight. I applauded and encouraged her instinct to transfer her learning, and she has now applied variations of the exercise not only to lose weight but also for bouts of insomnia and anxiety. With self-hypnosis, she has chosen a way to add to her own sense of self.

Choice is empowerment, and the sense of control that grows from making realistic choices that are supportive of ourselves can lead us to a place where it is possible to function more fully and with a great gain in pleasure, freedom, and a sense of personal optimism. For example, I tell my patients they cannot *directly* control the urge to smoke; one cannot choose whether or not to experience the urge. However, the *act* of placing a cigarette in your mouth and lighting it is a choice. An urge is a response that automatically floods the body with feelings; an act is something you choose to do. You can choose to smoke or choose not to smoke. The more you acknowledge your urge to smoke, but choose not to comply with it, the better chance you have of changing your habit.

When we are motivated, self-hypnosis supports our ability to choose and to change, and through self-hypnosis we can come to understand how we can be our own best physician. In an interview conducted with Dr. Albert Schweitzer in the 1950s, Norman Cousins asked Schweitzer how cures can occur outside of traditional medical practice. Schweitzer answered,

"Each patient carries his own doctor inside him. They come to us not knowing that truth. We are at our best when we give the doctor who resides within each patient a chance to go to work."

I found myself testing Schweitzer's theory with one of my first patients, Marcus, who was extremely skeptical of hypnosis and entirely unaware of the power within him to promote his own healing and recovery.

Chapter 2

SELF-HYPNOSIS IN PREPARATION FOR SURGERY:

A Technique for Promoting Healing and Reducing Risk

IN MARCH of 1978, Herbert Spiegel received a call from a surgeon in the cardiology unit at Columbia-Presbyterian Hospital. Marcus, a VIP biochemist, had been brought into the hospital for an emergency quadruple bypass and had asked to see a hypnotist. At the time, Spiegel was affiliated with Columbia University as a clinical professor, but his schedule was crowded with patients, lectures, and research. He told the surgeon I was at Columbia and that he should bring me in.

After discussing the case with Spiegel, I went to the university library to review the literature on the use of hypnosis in surgical situations, where I was particularly struck by an article in the *International Journal of Clinical and Experimental Hypnosis* by Dr. William Gruen. Gruen had prepared himself for bypass surgery by using progressive relaxation and suggestion. According to his surgeons, Gruen's medical progress was at the upper limit of recovery, and his preparations appeared to promote his rapid and comfortable convalescence. He reported feelings of tranquility and optimism five days before surgery and immediately after—even while he was unable to function without help or special effort. The article gave me some ideas. I then telephoned the surgeon at Columbia-Presbyterian Hospital—a world-renowned man in his field who had performed many bypass operations —and asked what he expected of me. He said, "You do your thing, I'll do mine, and we won't get in each other's way."

The first question I asked the patient, Marcus, was what he hoped to achieve from hypnosis. He proceeded to tell me that his daughter was dating a young man at Harvard Medical School whose father was a member of the American Society of Clinical Hypnosis. The father had advised Marcus to keep an open mind. "Hypnosis has worked for many people in your situation. What have you got to lose? It can't hurt you and it may help." That was Marcus's basis for requesting hypnosis when he checked into the hospital. Mincing no words, he told me he didn't believe for a minute that hypnosis would make any difference. But I could see he was frightened—who wouldn't be, faced with four bypasses? Marcus was obviously willing to try anything that might help.

The first step in the hypnosis process was to evaluate Marcus's capacity for trance. I did this by using Spiegel's Hypnotic Induction Profile, commonly called the HIP, which is a 5- to 10-minute formal clinical evaluation of hypnotic capacity. Marcus was extremely low, hovering somewhere between a grade Zero and a grade One, and it certainly didn't help that he was also flat-out skeptical. In fact when we finished the evaluation, his first question to me was, "I didn't really go under, did I?" I explained to him that different people respond to hypnosis in different ways, that it's not like the movies; you don't have to be "out" for hypnosis to be effective. I told him I observed a certain "letting go"—relaxed facial muscles, shoulder relaxation, head droop—adding up to the condition we call hypnosis. I also told him that only about 5 to 15 percent of the population are capable of entering the state of trance people think of as "going under," and that this state was not necessary for the therapy to work.

When I left Marcus on Monday afternoon (24 hours before his scheduled operation), he was still anxious but said he would do the 90-second exercise I had prescribed for him. He was to do it about once an hour until bedtime, then again hourly after awakening and until they wheeled him into the surgical chamber. He was to continue doing the exercise when he awoke from the anesthetic. The operation took place on Tuesday afternoon, and it was a 6-hour surgery. Earlier, the surgeon had said I could go up to the Intensive Care Unit (ICU), so at 7:30 Wednesday morning, I arrived at Columbia-Presbyterian's ICU—a place I had never visited before. Having been trained as a research psychologist without any background at a medical school, I was surprised at the size of the room. There were at least 150 beds, most of them occupied with patients. As I looked around the room, there was only one postoperative patient sitting up in bed, and it was Marcus. The sight of him—so alert—startled me. He looked entirely too healthy.

When I stood beside his bed, his first words to me were: "You hypnotists have lousy public relations. I feel ready to go home." Indeed, he looked ready to go home. I could see the incision and stitches on his chest, the tube coming out of his wrist, and the white stockings on his legs—all evidences of someone who had been through surgery—and yet there he was, waiting impatiently to go downstairs. He had to stay in the ICU, though, because there was no bed available; the hospital had not expected him to be ready to move for at least another day.

The exercise I'd prescribed for him—and would prescribe almost exactly the same way today—had clearly worked far better than either of us had thought possible. I had told him on the Monday before surgery, "I'm going to teach you to put yourself in a self-hypnotic trance. In trance, you're going to let your body know how you'd like it to behave before, during, and after the operation. You can use self-hypnosis, in addition to the usual medication, to prepare yourself for surgery.

"To enter trance, start by making yourself comfortable. Then follow the three-step procedure we will do together now.

"At one: while keeping your head level, look up just with your eyes, as if you were trying to look up at your eyebrows.

"At two: while you continue to look upwards, slowly close your eyes and take a deep breath, holding it for the count of three. One . . . two . . . three.

"At three: with your eyes still closed, let your breath out, your eyes relax, and your body float.

"You can imagine, if you like, that you're on a safe, comfortable white cloud, or a soft, feathery couch, and you can let your whole body float down, safe, relaxed . . . very comfortable. As you concentrate on this feeling of floating, I want you to think about the following things—you've come into the hospital so you and your surgeon can work together to cure your illness. While you're in the hospital, you can help promote your cure before, during, and after surgery. You help by letting your body know how to behave during treatment.

"There's a two-step exercise you can do to help yourself. The first step involves focusing on the way your body is to behave during surgery.

"Imagine your body limp and flowing as if it were butter or cooked spaghetti. You know you're being closely observed by skilled doctors and you can safely relax.

"There will be one part of you, though, that stays alert during surgery. That part is your body's protective system. That system can keep the wound dry, clean, and free of infection. It can also minimize bleeding, reduce discomfort, and promote healing. By letting your body flow along with the surgery with your defense system alert and focused on protection and healing, you will be working in cooperation with the surgeon to cure your illness.

"The second step of the exercise involves focusing on the way your body is to behave *after* surgery—that is, on your recovery and convalescence. Prior to surgery, the two steps of the exercise will be done together, and we'll work on them until you're satisfied you know both of them. Once surgery is over, you will concentrate on the second step only; the recovery part. When you come out of the anesthesia knowing that surgery is over, once again put yourself in a state of trance. Focus on alerting your defense system to promote healing. Keep the wound dry, clean, and free of infection. Minimize bleeding and reduce discomfort. Concentrate on a rapid return to normal functioning, to a stable and comfortable blood pressure. Imagine yourself getting hungry, feeling thirsty, going to the toilet. Think about getting back to a welcome lifestyle as your body heals.

"Thus far you've thought about the way your body is to behave during your stay in the hospital. Now I want you to think about the most important behavior. I want you to imagine the things you will do, without pain or worry, once you've recovered. I want you to imagine yourself doing the things you're eager to do. That's the reason you've come for surgery. You've come to repair a part of your body that is troubling you so you can do the things you want to do, without fear and concern.

"For a minute, think about what I've said and then I'll teach you how to bring yourself out of trance so that all of these messages stay with your body."

After a pause I had continued, saying, "Before I show you how to come out of trance, let's take the time to review your exercise. The first step focuses on the way your body is to behave during surgery; the second, on the way your body is to behave after surgery. Before surgery, you do both steps. After surgery, you do only the second step.

"In the first step, you think about the way your body is to behave during surgery. It is to be relaxed and limp, except for the defense system. That system is alert in order to keep the wound dry, clean, and free of infection, and to minimize bleeding and reduce discomfort. Although the anesthesiologist will provide whatever amount of anesthesia your body requires, you can make it easier by letting your body know the way to behave; help it flow along with the surgery so you and the surgeon work together to cure your illness.

"The second step focuses on recovery. Your defense system is alert to keep the wound dry, clean, and free of infection, and to minimize bleeding and reduce discomfort as the healing takes place. Imagine yourself as you regain all normal functioning—your blood pressure rapidly stabilizes and returns to normal. You feel your appetite return. You get thirsty. You sense yourself going to the toilet. You feel eager to move around. Each time before you come out of trance think about the future—the real reason for going through surgery. Imagine yourself doing things that you want to do once surgery is over and you have recovered."

I had paused again before saying, "To bring yourself out of trance, use a three-step procedure. Count backwards from three to one.

"At three: get ready, do it now.

"At two: with your eyes still closed, look all the way up.

"At one: open your eyes slowly, permitting them to come into focus."

I had prescribed that Marcus practice his self-hypnosis exercise about once an hour, and even more often if he felt the desire or need. I had told him he might have a different experience each time he did the exercise. Sometimes it would be light and sometimes it would feel very deep. Depth was not important; the key was to do the exercise often.

I had explained that there is no way you can overdose on self-hypnosis exercises. I had instructed him to continue with the exercise leading up to surgery, and once he came out of anesthesia, to concentrate on the part of the exercise that focused on healing and recovery.

For me, Marcus's positive surgical experience was both exciting and unsettling. I called his surgeon at the first opportunity and asked him whether this recovery was typical or unusual. I had no experience and could not judge from one case, but the surgeon had handled hundreds of cases. He told me that in his mind there was no question the self-hypnosis therapy had affected the course of surgery; he added that Marcus's recovery rate was definitely above the ordinary.

Marcus's rapid progress continued, and he left the hospital a week ahead of schedule. Now my job was to absorb the full meaning of just what Marcus and I had accomplished together. Educated as a researcher and scientist, I was no practitioner of magic tricks, nor did I believe in them. Initially, I found it difficult to accept what I had seen with my own eyes, and yet there was no denying that an important event had taken place. Surely if someone as experienced as the surgeon confirmed that the self-hypnosis had made a difference, then we were onto something significant, and I wanted to know more.

Shortly after my work with Marcus, *The New York Times* ran an article about preoperative hospital procedures, and I noticed it just at the fortuitous moment when I was searching for answers. The article described how people are prepared for surgery. First they are given a sedative, and once in surgery, they are given two different types of drugs—an anesthetic that reduces physical sensations, including pain, and a muscle relaxant to keep the body from tensing up during the course of the operation. Assuming that Marcus's preparation was the same, I asked myself how hypnosis had made a difference in the way he responded to the surgery. Our bodies, I reasoned, cannot distinguish between a surgeon and a mugger. All the body knows is that it is being penetrated by a blade. The usual response—neither the best nor the healthiest but certainly the most natural—is for the body to fight back against the invasion.

Is it any wonder that the body usually reacts to the scalpel as though it's a knife wielded by an assassin? The body's reactions are primitive and protective, dating back to prehistoric times when an enemy who attacked you with a sharp instrument definitely meant you nothing but harm. From the body's perspective that is what surgery is like; someone with a sharp instrument is penetrating your body. Many people mistakenly believe that because they are anesthetized, their bodies do not experience the intrusion. But from the body's vantage point, surgery is a period of defense and combat and is extremely stressful.

Physiologist Hans Selye identifies three stages of the body's reaction to stress: alarm, resistance, and exhaustion. The first stage—alarm—involves the fight or flight response. A release of hormones causes an increase in heartbeat and respiration, an elevation in blood sugar levels, an increase in perspiration, dilated pupils, and slowed digestion. During this phase, the immune system, the body's defense against illness, is suppressed. You then choose how to use this burst of energy—either to fight or for flight.

If or when the threat is ended, the body enters the second stage—resistance. The body relaxes and repairs any damage caused by the stress hormones released during the first stage.

In the third stage—exhaustion—if the stressor, that is, the threat of danger, remains, the body cannot relax. It stays alert and is unable to repair the damage. Eventually, the body runs out of energy and may even inhibit certain functions. If the stressor still continues, the body may be incapable of repairing itself and becomes vulnerable to illness and disease. Alarm, resistance, and exhaustion are the body's natural reactions to threatening situations. They are responses that

25

evolved in a hostile environment, and if they occur during surgery, are inappropriate and may even be dangerous.

Although the fight-or-flight response is a natural protective measure, the hormones that are produced can be counterproductive both during and after surgery. Pain, fear, and intrusion increase the heart rate, inhibit the protective immune response, create tension in the skeletal muscles, and affect blood flow. These changes are counter to what the body needs. After surgery, the tension may continue—bringing the body to exhaustion and therefore seriously reducing its capacity to heal itself.

Hypnosis provides us with tools for mediating the body's experience before and during surgery. Research shows that hypnosis allows us to reduce anxiety and fear, and, during surgery, to divert blood from an open wound, to reduce heart rate, muscle tension and pain, and to heighten immune system protection. After surgery, hypnosis can be used to relax the body, reduce pain, increase the flow of blood to injured muscle and tissue, and promote healing. The body heals itself.

A major component of the exercise I had created for Marcus was for him to talk to his body during trance and instruct it to flow along with the surgeon's scalpel. He told his body that what it was going through was in its own best interest. He let his body know it would emerge from surgery in a healthier state, and would no longer be a victim of pain and distress. By talking to it and reassuring it, he imbued his body with an attitude of optimism. Thus instead of a six-hour battle ensuing between the patient and the surgeon, there were six hours of synergism, of flowing along.

Throughout my years of practice, I have observed that the patients who use self-hypnosis require less anesthesia and muscle relaxant (both potentially toxic substances that can affect the organs), and are also far more successful at combatting stress. I have also observed that the patients who have used self-hypnosis tend to end up with the thinnest scars. It is as though the scalpel, when entering the body, cuts through soft, flowing tissue rather than tense tissue that is bound to rip.

When I later did research with Marsha Greenleaf, a health psychologist at New York's Albert Einstein College of Medicine, we identified a number of studies that showed that patients treated with hypnosis and suggestion benefited in a variety of ways. Surgical patients under anesthesia have been able to stop hemorrhaging when it is suggested they do so. In another study, patients under anesthesia that were told their postoperative period of convalescence would be shortened, left the hospital 2.42 days sooner than a comparative group of patients. Fred T. Koulouch, a surgeon at the University of Utah Medical School, used hypnotic techniques with 254 of his surgical cases to foster analgesia, anesthesia, and muscular relaxation. Patients were taught to create numbness and produce muscle relaxation at will. The majority of his patients required fewer postoperative treatments with pain medication, and left the hospital earlier than a comparative control group.

Other researchers report that suggestions given under hypnosis before surgery are useful in combatting specific fears and promoting the patient's peace of mind leading to surgery, and also postoperatively promote wound healing for a shorter and smoother convalescence. Research has shown that the use of hypnosis as preparation for surgery has, on rare occasions, achieved an unexpected therapeutic result.

Three doctors at University of California Los Angeles Medical School reported the successful treatment of a patient with severe upper gastrointestinal bleeding. She was admitted to the hospital with cold extremities, a rapid, "thready" pulse, and a dangerously high level of blood loss. A surgical resident discussed with the attending physician the possibility of helping the patient with hypnosis in order "to reduce her bleeding until we take her to the operating room." The patient at that point was pale, agitated, breathing rapidly—40 times a minute—shivering, and horrified by her state of body and mind. She accepted the idea of hypnosis willingly, and in her hypnosis session she was asked to think of pleasant memories from her past . . . of a beach perhaps . . . cool sand under her back, a cool breeze on her face . . . an ice-cold drink in hand . . . the happy laughter of children playing nearby.

She was told that her unconscious controlled her breathing and her pulse . . . that they would slow down . . . watch how deep and slow they are now . . . your unconscious mind is in control of your skin vessels, your blood pressure . . . it is taking good care of your body . . . you can allow it to control your bleeding completely. It will cool down and close all the bleeding points in your stomach and esophagus effectively and safely . . .

The patient's color gradually became better and she looked completely relaxed and calm. Her breathing slowed to normal, her blood pressure and heart rate dropped dramatically. It was suggested to her that she would be able to relax herself in this same manner and let her unconscious take care of her whenever she felt the need for it.

The doctors report that:

> In a stressful situation, this patient was highly motivated to accept hypnosis as a sure and safe method of treatment. A friendly reassuring approach was a welcome alternative to the hasty, worried, and mysterious atmosphere of the intensive care unit and the several hospital investigational procedures. The seriousness of her situation was made clear to her (perhaps exaggerated) by her transfer from one hospital to another, by her previous experience with similar attacks that led to major surgery, and by the multiple consultations on her condition.

> Consequently, she entered a fairly deep somnambulistic trance with little help from us, and her acceptance of our suggestion to stop the bleeding was quite impressive. Before her discharge, she pointed at the attending physician and said to one of her visitors, 'This is the doctor who saved my life.' She believed that what hypnosis, did for her was more important and more helpful than all the other procedures.

I have sometimes been asked how self-hypnosis can work if the patient has been put "under" by general anesthesia. As the obstetrician David B. Cheek has observed, sensory information and the resulting physical and muscular reactions are not totally interrupted by general anesthesia and muscle relaxants. Memory traces of what happened while the patient was "under" have been recalled during hypnotic regression. When consciousness is lost, the more primitive parts of the brain become acutely sensitive to any sensory information that describes the environment, and preoperative hypnotic suggestions can play a vital role during the actual period of surgery.

There is also evidence that patients under general anesthesia can hear. For example in a study of 33 patients undergoing surgery reported in 1985 in the *British Journal of Anaesthesiology*, patients were divided into either a suggestion or control group. Under established clinical levels of anesthesia, the suggestion group of patients were told to touch their ear during an interview they would have after the surgery was completed. When questioned later, the suggestion group was completely amnesic about being told to touch their ear; nonetheless, compared to the controls, they touched their ear much more frequently.

Remarkably, in my clinical practice to date, I have not had a single negative reaction to the use of self-hypnosis, either from patients or physicians. On the contrary, most patients who enter the trance state and create an exercise to help themselves are admonished by the nurses to slow down and take it easy once they are in recovery. Many patients have reported to me that they seem to recover more rapidly than their surgeon's other patients who rely primarily on drugs.

A patient of mine—Hugh, a television executive—benefited from self-hypnosis before surgery. Hugh had an acute stomach problem that turned into peritonitis. As a result, a section of his large intestine had to be removed. Here is his story in his own words.

"I was in great pain and was rushed to New York Hospital, but there were no beds and for a while it was touch and go as to whether I would be admitted. The doctor who operated on me was George Wantz, and as I was wheeled into the operating room, I said in a burst of terrified gallows humor, 'I certainly hope Wantz is enough.' It was—he was—and I survived. Following the procedure I was given a colostomy. About five months passed; the bag was going to be removed and I was going to be put back together.

"*Another* operation—I was frightened to death! I heard about Dr. Fisher's work from a friend who believed that self-hypnosis would help me recover quickly. Now I'm a rather feisty fellow; I hate inactivity almost as much as I hate hospitals. I was also damn scared.

"So I went to Stan and he taught me the technique of breathing, helped me shape an exercise, and suggested I take a mantra. I picked Peewee Reese, the former Brooklyn Dodger shortstop and one of my boyhood heroes. Stan also explained the theory of the flight-or-fight response. He told me that when the involuntary, or sympathetic, nervous system is evoked, certain hormones are secreted that can spike your blood pressure and heart rate. To counter that response, what I kept saying to myself over and over again was, 'The doctors are on my team. When they stick the knife in me, they don't intend to kill me. They plan to make me better.'

"The night before the operation, Stan came to my room and we turned out the lights for a coaching session. I crossed my arms over my shoulders and started to go into a trance when a resident came by and demanded to know what was going on. Why were the lights off? Who was the stranger sitting beside my bed while I kept mumbling, 'Peewee Reese, Peewee Reese?' Angry at the interruption, I told him we were doing voodoo and also told him to get lost. 'This is my doctor,' I said, motioning to Stan, 'and you're breaking my spell.'

"The next morning I was wheeled up to the operating room, breathing in and out—deep, relaxing breaths—and mumbling, 'Peewee Reese, Peewee Reese,' and telling myself that the surgeon was on my side. Before I went under, my doctor brought over an Oriental gentleman in a green smock and introduced him as a surgeon from Peking who was there to observe. Knowing that the Chinese are into acupuncture and other forms of exotic medicine, I said, 'Doctor, do I have something to tell *you*.' I quickly explained Stan's theory and told him I was doing it now and it was helping me, but even so, I was still plenty scared. I asked him to hold my hand. I went onto the table holding the hand of a Chinese surgeon from Peking and mumbling, 'Peewee Reese, Peewee Reese,' and feeling not half bad under the circumstances.

"I recovered and was out of the hospital in record time. And most important of all, I felt wonderful! The operation was a total success, and today I'm as good as new. I realize that from a scientific point of view there's no way to have a control on what Stan and the other successful medical hypnotists are doing, but I think it works. Hell, I *know* it works. It's a truism that most people as they grow older resent change, they think the new is never as good as the old. But self-hypnosis is one new thing that can truly help mankind."

Most people would agree with Hugh that hypnosis is a relatively new form of therapy; the fact is, however, it has been around at least since the 1830s when a Scottish surgeon, James Esdaile, became excited by its potential. In those days, the use of chemical anesthesia was rare and also dangerous; the doctor administered alcohol or had the patient restrained during surgery. Esdaile, however, performed more than 3,000 witnessed surgeries (over 300 hundred of these were major), using the hypnotic approach developed by Austrian physician, Franz Anton Mesmer, as the sole anesthetic.

One of the common major surgical procedures in Esdaile's practice was the removal of scrotal tumors, which had a mortality rate during that era of 50 percent. With Esdaile's use of hypnosis for patient preparation, the mortality rate in 161 cases was only five percent.

Esdaile wrote a report on his work, brought it back to England, and presented it to the British Medical Society. Esdaile's report was criticized by colleagues who felt his patients were faking. The society's president, however, was convinced of the technique's efficacy and was eager to promote its use in surgery. Many members of the society were nervous about his recommendation, and forcefully disclaimed the scientific nature of hypnosis. However, many surgeons in England and France began using hypnosis as an anesthesia until it was replaced by the use of chemical anesthesia in 1848.

Hypnosis stayed in the doldrums until the late nineteenth century. Then, other medical uses of hypnosis began to be popularized. An 1892 report for the British Medical Society acknowledged hypnotism as beneficial, and encouraged its use for insomnia, pain, alcoholism, and many functional disorders. An 1890 article in the *Journal of the American Medical Association* praised the use of hypnosis as "a valuable therapeutic agent . . . in suitable cases and in proper hands." M. H. Lackersteen, M.D., who had seen the work of the mesmeric hospitals in Calcutta and witnessed operations done under mesmerism, wrote

Hypnotism is a fact which is sure to be more generally appreciated the better it is known and understood . . . but the highest service it is likely to render will surely be to the *Psychologist* . . . By hypnotic suggestion the psychologist of the future will in one single year learn more of the mind and the mechanism of its so-called faculties than the highest talent of the world had been able to ascertain in two thousand years.

Cures of physical and functional illnesses were reported by Amboise Auguste Liebeault, a physician, and Hippolyte Marie Bernheim, professor of medicine at the Nancy Clinic in France, who used hypnosis in his treatment of patients. Sigmund Freud, who studied with Bernheim and Jean Martin Chacot, a clinical neurologist, used it in the treatment of hysterical illness hoping it could help patients recover the repressed emotions of early traumatic experiences. But, Freud's interest waned when he found that not all of his patient's were equally "susceptible" to hypnosis. The belief in the late 1800s was that it was the hypnotherapist, rather than the patient, who controlled the trance experience. There were many failures. Freud's waning interest, coupled with the widespread disappointment in hypnosis as a permanent cure for hysteria, nearly succeeded in dealing hypnosis a death blow shortly after the turn of the century. The number of scientific articles and books devoted to hypnosis—once numbering in the thousands annually—dwindled to several dozen a year.

The First World War changed all that. Servicemen suffered from a grim variety of war neuroses—muscle spasms, paralysis and amnesia, among others. Because of the shortage of psychiatrists and the need for a condensed form of therapy, hypnosis was revived and used for the relief of traumatic neuroses. World War II brought about an even greater employment of hypnosis as a short-term therapeutic procedure, and success in the treatment of war neuroses created a new climate of enthusiasm for hypnosis.

What's more, 150 years after Esdaile, it's being used once again in special instances as the sole anesthesia during surgery. Although not for everyone, it has proved to be a useful alternative for some patients who cannot be safely treated with conventional anesthesia techniques. The *Journal of the American Medical Association* reports an interesting case of a 40-year-old, extremely obese woman whose doctors relied solely on hypnoanaesthesia for the surgical removal of a large tumor from her thigh region. The position of the lesion and her obesity made general anesthetic or a spinal impossible. Over a three-week period, two psychologists trained her in self-hypnosis, and the anesthesiologist "rehearsed" her on the step-by-step surgical procedure she would undergo. The procedure was successful in this case, although the doctors were clear to emphasize its rarity as a choice of treatment, noting that at most, 10 percent of patients are able to tolerate surgery under hypnosis without any chemical assistance. Although there is ample evidence in the scientific literature showing that major surgery can be performed with the patient under hypnosis, the extent to which it can be used as the sole anesthesia with a serious surgical procedure remains an area of controversy.

Indeed, many medical hypnotists question whether a surgical patient can use self-hypnosis effectively enough on his own to maintain the pain-free level of comfort and relaxation required during surgery. In most studies reported in the literature (including the one cited above) the patient does not usually induce and maintain the trance state without assistance. A psychologist or medical hypnotist is present during the operation as part of the surgical team. In opposition, Victor Rausch, a Canadian dental surgeon, considers the limits described by the literature on the effectiveness of self-hypnosis in major surgery to be academic and unfounded. A cholecystectomy (or removal of the gall bladder) was performed on him in which self-hypnosis was the sole anesthetic agent. Muscle relaxation, shallow breathing, pulse rate, blood pressure, reflex action, and pain were successfully controlled during and following surgery. Rausch shared his reasons for choosing such an unconventional, even controversial approach in an article in the *American Journal of Clinical Hypnosis*. He wrote:

> The reason I chose self-hypnosis as my mode for anesthesia was a selfish one. I had a burning curiosity and desire to experience first-hand the mental changes that would have to occur within myself if the procedure was to be successful. I also wanted to learn, if not objectively, at least subjectively, about some of the mechanisms involved in self-hypnosis, and determine if I could act both as operator and subject effectively. I wanted to discover to what extent I could control my body through the use of self-hypnosis, and was prepared to take the risk . . .
>
> During the hour and fifteen minutes that I was on the operating table, I was able to achieve the depth of hypnosis necessary for the procedure to be completely successful. I was able to critically make judgments and alter and direct my hypnotic approaches during each step of the operation. At all times my critical faculty was active. I was

amazed at how effectively self-hypnosis was working but I could not explain to myself how it was working. I knew, perhaps intuitively, what images I had to form mentally and what feelings I had to elicit to produce the desired results. I became 'stronger' whenever I had eye contact with either the nurse or the anesthetist, and my ability to manipulate and control various physiological functions increased as the operation progressed.

The operation was totally successful and no difficulties arose before, during, or after surgery.

Whereas self-hypnosis as the sole anesthesia would be a scary perspective for most people, its use as a preparation for surgery, though still not commonly prescribed, has been comfortably accepted by patients and has led to its application in other situations. Another patient of mine, Rachel, asked for help first for her 15-year-old son, whose jaw had to be broken and reset to eliminate a protrusion that affected his bite—a procedure requiring that his mouth be wired shut for six weeks. Being young and facing both confinement and pain, Danny was experiencing a high degree of stress. His self-hypnosis exercise helped him understand that he was going through a difficult experience for the best of reasons: to help himself. It was a present he was giving himself. He was going to look better and feel better as a result of the operation. He was empowering himself by knowing he could deal with the experience; he was growing into a stronger, more optimistic person.

Rachel was pleased with the results. Danny went through the procedure and the postoperative healing in excellent fashion. Now, suffering from a problem of her own, she decided to turn to me. As she says in her own words, "A little more than a year ago, I needed an emergency hysterectomy. I felt that self-hypnosis sessions with Stan would help, and my surgeon didn't object. In the financial world—my world—the biggest problem is always downside risk, and the beauty of this procedure is that it has no downside risk at all. You can't die from too much self-hypnosis, nor can you be allergic to it. It's really very reassuring to know you can only be the beneficiary.

"Stan worked with me on the exercise he'd created for me for an hour in the hospital the night before the operation. The next day I needed two transfusions to bring my blood levels up, and I kept doing the exercise religiously. When I got into the operating room, I told the anesthesiologist that perhaps I wouldn't need as much anesthesia as he usually gives. He said he was very happy to hear that and promised me he would watch himself to make sure he didn't treat me like the average patient. I also told him I'd had problems with nausea in the past whenever I needed a general anesthetic. He told me times had changed and the anesthesia was better now. So I really can't tell if it was purely self-hypnosis—a component of my exercise was aimed at combatting nausea—or the fact that better drugs are used now, or maybe a combination of the two factors. All I know is, I had a truly positive experience instead of a horrifying one.

"When I came out, I was in the next bed to a woman who was about 30. I'm 51. She had the same doctor, the same surgery, and on the sixth day she was still taking pain killers. I took them for the first 24 hours, when they give them almost automatically. Anyway, the pain is so bad at first that you need a lot, but even then I don't think I needed as much as most. After the first day, I relied on my exercise, and the difference was absolutely extraordinary. I left the hos-

pital after six days while this woman 20-some yea
my junior was still swallowing pain killers.

"There's nothing magical about self-hypnosis
either. It's a thought process. It's displacing stress or
pain with a receptive quality—a series of positive,
healing thoughts and images. I think this is the sort of
natural technique that allows the peasant woman to
give birth in the fields. I know it carried me through
the childbirth of my three sons, without my even
knowing at the time I was using self-hypnosis. Now,
for me, it's become a learned technique that lessens
the pain in my teeth when I'm in the dentist's chair,
whereas before I used it, I would grip the chair arms
until my fingers screamed with pain.

"What I'm saying is, many of us practice self-
hypnosis as a natural process of living. Now I can call
on it at will. I've learned it. What the exercise does is
displace pain with a mind-set and an intensity of
thought that's a lot more sensible than gripping the
dentist chair and feeling so much tension you hurt
yourself.

"Basically, thanks to self-hypnosis, I came to feel
before the operation that the surgeon was not coming
at me with a knife to butcher me; he was going to
make wonderful and whole what was sick and bad at
the time. And that sort of thinking is very, very important. It's the kind of thinking—loving and protective
of yourself, and at the same time, very sane—that can
begin to reshape your entire life."

Of course it cannot be said too often that self-
hypnosis does not work all the time and for all people.
It is an imperfect technique, like all techniques. The
procedures involve an element of trial and error, and
we would all benefit from having a broader research
base. The strong strain of skepticism on the part of

medical scientists, though, is belied by the case studies and research projects done over the past several decades. These studies show that preoperative hypnosis and suggestions given under anesthesia have a positive influence on the recovery process. The advantages reported in these studies are:

1. Reduction in the normally required amounts of anesthesia and pain killers.
2. Cessation of hemorrhaging and a reduction in blood loss.
3. More rapid wound healing.
4. Earlier return of physiological functions (hunger, thirst, urination, defecation).
5. Reduction in fear, apprehension and anxiety.
6. Shorter convalescence.

Despite the scientific support for hypnosis in preparation for—and even during—surgery, its use in a hospital setting is still unfortunately the exception rather than the rule. Patients are prepared for—and treated during—surgery pretty much as in the past.

Although many physicians will privately acknowledge that hypnosis may work—at least for some patients—they find it professionally difficult to make referrals. They recoil from any formal affiliation with hypnosis. This does not prevent them from letting their patients use it, and privately they are cooperative about allowing a professional who employs hypnosis to work with them. The problem is, hypnosis is simply too "magical" for their taste. It has never entirely lived down its reputation as being somewhat disreputable or fraudulent.

Because the clinical application of self-hypnosis to surgery proved effective in case after case in my private practice, I decided to become an active participant in the campaign to win over more medical professionals and conduct a formal research project on my own. I knew I would need to locate a surgeon and an institution in the New York City area where I lived that would provide access to surgical patients so I could develop a scientific approach to understanding the technique. After a year of queries and rejections, I met in January 1981 with Thomas King, Professor of Surgery at Columbia-Presbyterian, and Steven Rosenberg, Area Health Department Chief. Both expressed interest and were willing to help.

King proposed as a research strategy that we work with open-heart surgery patients. He explained that in that particular type of surgery—a Coronary Artery Bypass Graft (CABG)—the procedures seldom vary. They are so well established the professionals describe a coronary artery by-pass as "cookie cutter" surgery.

I agreed that this type of surgery would be an ideal method for studying the effect of self-hypnosis in the management of surgical cases. First of all, because the surgical procedure for bypass surgery is so standardized, a respectable research protocol could be developed. Second, if the research demonstrated that self-hypnosis made a difference, the results would be taken seriously. King offered to approach some cardiologists and try to enlist their support for the project. Earlier, a prominent cosmetic surgeon had shown interest in the self-hypnosis technique after I had worked with one of his patients; but I felt that results in that arena would be viewed less urgently by the medical community than if I concentrated the research on patients with life-threatening conditions.

Months passed. King called to apologize—an apology which by now was growing all-too familiar.

He explained that although there was some interest in the project, he had not been able to get a commitment or access to a patient population. It was another year before the opportunity finally did arrive. In 1982, I met with Jack Wilder, Associate Dean of the Albert Einstein School of Medicine. Wilder had read my project proposal and thought it was a possibility if I could work with a Ph.D. candidate in health psychology.

The candidate, Marcia Greenleaf, (now a practicing psychologist) was an experienced practitioner who used hypnosis to treat patients at the college hospital. She and I immediately hit it off and started to plan the research. It was she who connected us with Robert Frater, Chief of CardioThoracic Surgery, and asked for his help with the project. Frater and the Supervising Anesthesiologist, Yasu Oka, thought we should observe them in surgery before discussing the project, which we did several weeks later.

After watching the preparation and bypass operation for seven hours, I described to Frater what we hoped to accomplish. He asked me why I was convinced self-hypnosis would work, and I told him my theory that the body did not distinguish between a surgeon and a mugger. I told him that by using self-hypnosis we could help the patient's body understand that the surgeon's function was to help, not hurt, that he was a healer, not a mugger. I told him that self-hypnosis could help the patient flow along with the surgery rather than fight it. Surgeons and anesthesiologists had told us that the bodies of patients who used self-hypnosis are very relaxed during surgery. Frater's eyes lit up. He said he had wondered since the days of his surgical residency why the patient's body, no matter how sedated and anesthetized, would tense whenever the scalpel entered. He and Oka offered their support for the research, and we were on our way.

Despite the variety of problems that typically occur in the early stages of experimental research, we were able to collect evidence that produced two major findings. We found that *a patient's hypnotic capacity affects his response to surgery and recovery*—specifically that patients with medium capacities recovered more rapidly than those with either low or high capacities. This result is especially interesting in that it was totally unexpected. Until further studies are done, we can only speculate as to why this occurred.

We also found that *suggestions given during self-hypnosis can affect a patient's physiological responses.* Patients directed to totally relax during the pre and postoperative phases produced more fluid drainage than either the control group or the self-hypnosis group guided to keep the wound *dry* and clean. Even these pilot-study findings are an indication that self-hypnosis, appropriately applied, can influence the natural course of surgery and recovery.

Progress, however, has been slow. Unfortunately, the use of self-hypnosis in a hospital setting is still rare. Up to the present time, I've worked with perhaps 300 surgery patients—a drop in the bucket when you consider that in this country alone there are 300,000 bypass surgeries performed each year, as well as probably 650,000 hysterectomies, and 2,500,000 other major surgeries. (According to the National Center for Health Statistics, more than 39,192,000 in-hospital surgical procedures were performed in 1988.) It seems realistic to argue that we could help a significant percentage of these patients have a less stressful surgery, require lower doses of toxic chemicals, and achieve a much more rapid rate of recovery if self-hypnosis as preparation for surgery were more actively prescribed.

The experiences of many of my patients confirm this. When I meet with them before surgery, regardless of their condition, they tend to be fearful. They fear needles, anesthesia, pain, and loss of control. Some of them have had bad experiences with surgery in the past and have to fight against distrust. Others are concerned about a successful return to normal functioning and mobility. My patients who have used self-hypnosis as preparation for surgery have run the gamut of physical problems, including mastectomy, coronary artery bypass, breast and jaw reconstruction, ovarian cyst removal, hip replacement, tumor removal, angiogram, root canal, hysterectomy, colon and intestinal cancer, skin graft, brain tumor, and childbirth. Regardless of the severity and type of problem, they all benefited from its use.

I can offer my own experience as one piece of empirical evidence that self-hypnosis can approach frontiers not generally recognized by conventional medicine. A few years ago I was about to undergo surgery and was doing an exercise in preparation for it. I used the exercise before I went into the hospital and continued to use it as I readied myself for the operation. It was the first time I had used self-hypnosis, on myself for a medical problem and I asked the same questions my patients ask: Am I doing it effectively enough? Am I going deep enough? Is my concentration as pure as I can make it?

Fortunately, I had proof that it clearly was effective. Normally just before surgery, your anticipatory anxiety increases and your blood pressure can climb right off the chart. With me, it was the opposite. The closer I got to surgery, the more my blood pressure dropped. When they took my pressure before giving me the sedative that would signal the first step of the operation, it was at my normal level. The exercise proved to be effective before and during surgery, and my post operative recovery was well above average. I was helping myself and helping my body to help itself. My surgeon said there was no doubt in his mind that anyone who knew how to do these kinds of exercises would have a more benign course of surgery than otherwise, with less pain, less bleeding, and less swelling, and a much more rapid recovery.

Chapter 3

UNDERSTANDING THE TRANCE STATE:

The Power of Our Imagination

I AM often asked what literally takes place when you enter the trance state. First of all, there is a letting go —your body relaxes and your focus is inward. You are less aware of your surroundings.

There is a dullness to the phone as it rings. Street traffic and household noises seem remote. Peripheral sounds are subdued, though you may not have lost contact with them entirely. In this state, you can communicate clearly with your body, using all forms of memory—visceral, as well as verbal and visual. When you imagine a scene, some of you can see it in front of you and some may only feel it; most of us, however, can do both. If you are thinking of a hot summer's day, you can see the scene, feel the warmth, and recreate the experience in your body.

Without realizing it, you may already know what trance is like. Natural trance occurs during moments of intense concentration or creativity when, for example, a composer may have no recollection of having written a phrase. The notes seem to have arranged themselves. Or, an accountant may become so involved in his weekly business report he's unaware of the movement and noise around him. Moviegoers can become so engrossed in what is happening on the screen—their focus is so exclusively *there*—that they respond to events as though they are part of them and not a member of the audience.

Drivers have had the experience of being so preoccupied with something that they lose all sense of the road, the flow of traffic, and of whether or not they have passed other cars. Other natural trance communications can be as simple as skipping meals while deeply engrossed in solving a problem. Many of us have drifted into what is called a hypnagogic state just before we fall asleep or on slowly awakening—half in a dream, half awake, relaxed, peaceful, and in touch with ourselves. In this state we can often control and continue pleasant dreams.

What has happened? The composer, the accountant, the moviegoer, the driver, the person moving in a state somewhere between sleep and wakefulness—they have told their bodies that unless there's an emergency, all surrounding sights and sounds will be blocked out. For as long as the natural trance lasts, they stop responding to signals from the outer world, they are finely attuned to themselves and their own imaginations, and they are inwardly preoccupied and focused; they are in a state of self-hypnosis.

Stephen T. Gilligan writes that the

> trance state is biologically essential for all human beings . . . not only is trance experienced in many situations—daydreaming, dancing, listening to

music, reading a book, watching television—but it is also induced in many different ways. The trance can be induced through rhythmic and repetitive movement (dancing, running, rocking, breathing exercises, etc.); through chanting, meditation, prayer, group rituals, etc.; by focusing on an image, an idea, the sound of someone's voice; through relaxation, massage, warm baths, etc.; through drugs such as alcohol, cannabis, or tranquilizers. All of these methods tend to decrease the cacophony of conscious awareness with its discontinuous patterns of stimulation. Anthropologists have noted that trance rituals can be found in nearly every culture on the planet, and they have been around for centuries.

The psychologist Erica Fromm and her colleagues at the University of Chicago studied individual experiences with self-hypnosis. The subjects were taught a variety of techniques for entering into a trance and were asked to keep a journal of their experiences, recording in the journal the results of specific self-suggestions for the session and time spent in a state of inactivity. These are excerpts from the subjects' notes:

Donald—Day 11
Suggestions today: that I would smell a lemon without visualizing it first; that I would feel my legs and feet moving as if walking without visualizing anything; that I would smell freshly cut grass . . . and that I would taste a specific candy bar without visualizing it. Suggestions were successful.

Sarah—Day 15:
I began by asking why is it that I feel I must eat so much—where the compulsion to eat arose. The image that came to my mind was first a fuzzy

one of being in a cradle—that I saw myself as a little girl stealing cookies from the cookie jar in defiance of my mother. By stealing food I could rebel against her authority, but at the time I was punishing myself by being overweight . . . I began suggesting a way out of this, seeing that I have totally grown out of my mother's judicial range.

Louise—Day 20 (She had lost her husband the previous year and was using self-hypnosis to explore her loss.)

Suddenly felt myself in the hospital—with oxygen mask, IV, the whole thing (just like my husband). My breathing became heavy and painful, my chest hurt—I could feel my heart pounding. My body felt swollen and immovable . . . This whole vision was very vivid, the physical aspects were frighteningly real . . . in this reenactment there was a feeling that his death was, for him, an escape from an unbearable pain—there was no sadness. As I write this, I feel a great sadness for my loss—but in the imagery it was his feelings I was experiencing and they expressed the need to escape from that tortured body.

It should be pointed out, however, that natural trance can also have a destructive side. You can become so focused, so concentrated that you literally push yourself beyond healthy limits without even knowing it. For example, a patient of mine, Margaret, who is an exceptionally good hypnotic subject, often ignores signals from her body of hunger or fatigue. At dinner parties, she performs as if she's on stage; she never eats and the minute the party is over, she's totally wiped out from too much energy output and too little attention to the food. She has abused her body—

pushed it beyond its capacity to function properly—because she is neither aware she is doing it nor that she has the capacity to do it. People who are less hypnotizable are not as likely to fall into that trap. There are, therefore, advantages and disadvantages to both the low and high ends of the trance-ability spectrum, but if you understand who you are and make full use of whatever capacity you have, hypnosis can become very powerful.

Most people I meet, when they learn I work with hypnosis, ask me to describe the procedure I use. They ask how I decide if hypnosis will work, and what type of treatment is needed.

In answer, I will describe what it is some of my colleagues and I try to accomplish in a single, 45- to 50-minute evaluation and treatment session. Normally, I spend the first 20 minutes with a new patient learning why she has come to see me; to be helpful I need to understand the problem she wants to overcome and what she would like to see happen. I also need to understand what beliefs, feelings, or thoughts she holds that contribute to her problem. I look for a sense of who she is and what is important to her. Although the time frame is limited, there are a variety of problems susceptible to this short-term approach. If there are many problems or if the problem presented appears to be very complex, alternative approaches are explored. However, for many patients a single session is enough.

Before I begin the evaluation of the patient's hypnotic capacity, I ask what she feels or knows about hypnosis. A patient's knowledge is usually distorted by myth or superstition, which can create a certain level of anxiety. Most patients coming to see me for the first time are anxious about giving up control, and believe *they* cannot be hypnotized. I explain to the new patient that all hypnosis is really self-hypnosis and that the difference in the degree of hypnotizability does not limit the therapeutic use of the technique (as shown by Marcus' experience with surgery in Chapter 2).

Those who are more highly hypnotizable have a capacity to do some things others cannot do, but the ability to make use of hypnotic capacity is personal and you may be more effective in its use than someone with a higher capacity. Hypnotic capacity is similar to intelligence or talent; each one of us has a unique collection of talents and some of us learn how to maximize and use whatever gifts we have better than others.

In order to assess a patient's hypnotizability, I use the Hypnotic Induction Profile (the HIP), a clinical evaluation of hypnotic capacity, which is published in its entirety in *Trance and Treatment* by psychiatrists Herbert and David Spiegel. The HIP postulates that hypnosis is a subtle perceptual alteration involving a capacity for focused concentration that is inherent in the person and can be tapped by the examiner.

What I am about to describe is intended to familiarize you with the HIP evaluation procedure used by a professional. This procedure consists of a number of steps that, altogether, take no more than five to 10 minutes to administer. The Spiegels have emphasized the importance of following instructions for each step in the HIP *verbatim*, because the accuracy of the scores depend on the degree to which the phenomena described in the instructions are experienced and reported by the patient. Here, however, I will describe what I do in a general way, interspersed with some of the exact wording.

I begin the evaluation with the patient seated in a comfortable chair. I ask the patient to place her arms on the armrest and feet flat on the floor. I say, "Lean back and make yourself as comfortable as you can."

I then say, "Now look toward me, right at me. Hold your head level. As you hold your head in that position, look up toward your eyebrows—now, toward the top of your head."

The patient's head needs to be kept level, tilted neither up nor down, allowing me to measure the upward gaze.

"As you continue to gaze upward, close your eyelids slowly. That's right . . . Close. Close. Close."

When the lids are halfway closed, I note the position of the pupils. This gives me the eyeroll score, the best single predictor of hypnotic capacity. The more white of the eye that shows, the higher the score. This is the first step in the scoring procedure.

I continue.

"Keep your eyelids closed . . . continue to hold your eyes upward. Take a deep breath, hold. Now exhale, let your eyes relax while keeping the lids closed and let your body float. Imagine a feeling of floating, floating right down through the chair . . . There will be something pleasant and welcome about this sensation of floating."

People expect to float upward rather than downward, and the degree of ability to accept this paradox can tell the tester something about the subject's hypnotizability. At this point in the HIP, I am also getting the patient to pay close attention to my voice and instructions.

"As you concentrate on this floating, I'm going to concentrate on your right arm." (You can use either the right or left arm, depending on your seating arrangement.)

I now establish contact with the patient by placing her right arm, gently but firmly, on the arm of the chair. Touch is used to focus her attention on the physical sensations that may accompany verbal instructions. Touch also helps me to know how light or heavy, flexible or stiff, the patient's arm is—essential information for evaluating the patient's psychological disposition.

I then place my hand, gently but firmly, on the patient's wrist, a sign that I'm now going to employ touch as a form of instruction. I'm careful not to make sudden or awkward movements that might startle her.

"In a while, I'm going to stroke the middle finger of your right hand. After I do, you will develop movement sensations in that finger. Then the movements will spread, causing your right hand to feel light and buoyant, and you will let it float upward. Ready?"

I stroke the middle finger, then move along the hand and up along the forearm to the elbow pressing gently but firmly. Pressing down seems to create the opposite response; the patient's hand and forearm will usually move upward. If I get an immediate response, I then say, "Now I'm going to position your arm in this manner, so . . . And let it remain in this upright position." But if there is no hand levitation at that stage, I give this additional instruction: "First one finger, then another. As these restless movements develop, your hand becomes light and buoyant, your elbow bends, your forearm floats into an upright position."

At this point I give the patient's arm a light lift. This physical communication may work better for some patients than any verbal command. If the patient still has difficulty taking over upright movement,

I say, "Let your hand be a balloon. Just let it go. You have the power to let it float upward. That's right! Help it along! Just put it up there."

It is essential for the purpose of the HIP evaluation that the patient's hand and forearm go into the upright position, even if I have to tell the subject to put it up or guide it myself. When the forearm reaches the upright position, I say, "Now I'm going to position your arm in this manner, so . . . And let it remain in this upright position."

I then cup the patient's elbow with both hands, positioning it on the armrest of the chair and flexing the hand forward. I instruct the patient to let her arm remain in an upright position, to permit the hand to levitate after I pull it down, and to feel normal sensation return in response to my touching the right elbow. All of these instructions are given with the patient's eyes still closed and while her hand is in the instructed upright position.

"In fact," I then say, "your arm will remain in that position even after I give you the signal for your eyes to open. When your eyes are open, even after I put your hand down, it will float right back up to where it is now. You will find something amusing about this sensation. Later, when I touch your right elbow, your usual sensation and control will return.

"In the future, each time you give yourself the signal for self-hypnosis, at the count of one, your eyes will roll upward and by the count of three, your eyelids will close and you will feel in a relaxed trance state. Each time you will find the experience easier and easier.

"Now I am going to count backwards. At two, your eyes will again roll upward with your eyelids closed. At one, let them open very slowly. Ready . . . Three, two, with your eyelids closed, roll up your eyes and one, let them open slowly. All right, stay in this position and describe what physical sensations you are aware of now in your right arm and hand.

These are the instructions for leaving the formal trance ceremony, but only the induction ceremony has ended, not the trance itself. The patient, with her eyes now open, is in a state of postceremonial trance—a relaxed state of focused concentration.

I ask the patient if she is comfortable, or aware of any tingling sensation in her hand or arm. I then ask, "Does your right hand feel as if it is not as much a part of your body than your left hand?"

If the patient answers "No," I say, "Does your right hand feel as connected to the wrist as your left hand feels connected to the wrist? Is there a difference?"

I take the patient's right hand and gently lower it onto the arm of the chair. After 10 seconds of no movement of the hand, I say: "Now turn your head. Look at your right hand and watch what is going to happen." This is the first reinforcement for signalled arm levitation, and touching is not used at this stage.

The second reinforcement, given 10 seconds later, is, "While concentrating on your right hand, imagine it to be a huge, buoyant balloon."

The third reinforcement is, "Now, while imagining it to be a balloon, permit it to act out as if it were a balloon."

The fourth reinforcement is, "This is your chance to be a method actor or a ballet dancer. Think of your hand as a balloon or as the arm of a ballet dancer leaping gracefully through the air, and permit it to act as if it were a balloon. That's right—just put it up there, just the way a ballet dancer would."

I tell the patient to let her hand up, even if she has to "pretend."

Next I say, "While it remains in the upright position, by way of comparison, raise your left hand. Now put your left arm down. Are you aware of a difference in sensation in your left arm going up compared to your right? For example, does one arm feel lighter or heavier than the other?" If there is any difference in sensation, it has emerged from the trance experience, because the patient was not told beforehand to feel a difference. If there is one, it is *discovered during trance*.

I now say, "Are you aware of any relative difference in your sense of control in one arm compared to the other as it goes up?"

If the patient answers "Yes," which is the expected response, I say, "In which arm do you feel more control?" I record and score the response. If the patient answers "No," it indicates that the patient has distanced himself from the experience. That response is also recorded.

At this point, I cup the patient's right elbow with my left hand, touching both the inside and outside of the elbow; at the same time I gently grasp the patient's right wrist with my right hand and slowly lower her forearm and hand onto the arm of the chair, and say, "Make a tight fist, real tight, and now open it." This is the cut-off signal for the hand levitation.

I let go of the elbow with my left hand. With my right hand, I stroke the patient's right forearm by pressing down firmly, starting at the elbow and moving toward the fingertips, and say, "Before, there was a difference between the two forearms. Are you aware of any change in sensation now?"

At the word "now," I press the patient's right hand as a way of punctuating the end of stroking her

57

right arm. The point of this procedure is to restore normal sensation to the patient's right arm and to exit the postinduction trance program.

While I am scoring the patient's HIP evaluation, the patient has a few moments to reflect on her experience, often her first, with hypnosis. I then ask, "What was the experience like for you? Do you have any questions?" I tell patients their score in a range from zero to four, with four being the highest capacity. I explain that this evaluation assists us in devising a hypnotic exercise for them that maximizes their potential. I remind them that almost all patients, except for those with a zero score (which is rare) are candidates for self-hypnosis.

At this stage, patients are usually surprised to discover they were fully aware of what was happening, and could have stopped the procedure at any time. They also recognize how difficult it is simply to let go and engage the experience. They are surprised to discover they *are*, indeed, hypnotizable.

I point out that although nothing flowed from my eyes or fingers—or any other part of my body—their hand felt lighter. They took the suggestion that their hand would float and told their body to act and feel a sense of buoyancy. Physiologically, using their imagination and without knowing how, they tensed the muscles in their forearm; this caused the hand to float up and feel comfortable in an upright position.

A central component of the hypnotic condition is an acceptance of what would seem to be an entirely illogical situation. For example, during the induction I ask them to float "down, down through the chair." I tell them, "Your hand will become lighter and float into an upright position." Neither of these statements makes logical sense; what I have described is trance logic—a key component of the hypnotic experience.

Trance logic is the noncritical acceptance of an illogical circumstance. If, while working with age regression, I tell you you're getting younger and younger and you're now back in the year 1960, how can that be? After all, it is 1991 right now as I'm talking to you. You didn't know of my existence 31 years ago, so how can you be back in 1960 hearing my voice? And yet some of you will feel you are back in 1960 and can hear my voice. Trance logic permits you to accept a contradictory situation without the intervention of the ego defenses. You become more open and receptive to the flexibilities of ideas, time, and memory.

Through the acceptance of trance logic, you can exercise whatever capacity you have to reexperience key moments in your past. For example, Diane came to see me about her inability to remember events in her early childhood that involved her family. She was writing a novel in the form of a memoir and much of the text was to be highly autobiographical. She could recall only fragments about herself, her parents, and her two brothers in the period before her tenth birthday. She was worried that her amnesia, as she called it, would rob her work of richness. Her HIP evaluation showed that she was high in hypnotic capacity (she was a 4), and was capable of going back in time not merely as an observer but also to reexperience different aspects of her life in her earliest years. Through self-hypnosis, she was able to use visceral memory to relive an experience—complete with sights, smells, and emotions—as she had experienced it 30 years before. She could summon up the smell of the lilacs she, then six, had picked for her mother who lay in bed seriously ill with pneumonia. She could see Jack, the golden retriever, as he ran after sticks in the field behind the house where she lived. Although she had not thought of Jack in years, his smell came back to her as if, at the very moment of recall, her nose were buried in his fur. She was able to taste and smell the Thanksgiving feast prepared lovingly by her grandmother, and sensed the way she stuffed herself until her sides ached. This reexperiencing, with its rich flow of association and sensation, empowered her as a writer.

Reynolds Price's recent memoir, *Clear Pictures*, is a subtle and moving account of how, through the natural power of his own trance ability, he opened himself to larger dimensions of his being. In the foreword to *Clear Pictures*, Price describes a state of intense concentration—arrived at and experienced by the most natural of means—in which he managed to remove pain from his body and, at the same time, liberate his mind from its usual constraints in order to more fully create a portrait of his past. During an extended convalescence—he had undergone three operations for cancer of the spine—he began 10 weeks of training at Duke Hospital in the techniques of biofeedback and hypnosis. He says:

> My hypnotist was Dr. Patrick Logue; and he spent a good part of our first meeting in assuring me of the benign nature of hypnosis. I was able to assure him that, because of an enjoyable adolescent trance, induced by my tenth-grade biology teacher, I had no fears and was eager to start.
>
> In the remainder of that first hour—with only the doctor's level voice and his ample stock of verbal images for serenity, trust and the imaging of painful areas—I entered a quarter-hour state in which I was literally ecstatic, standing in high

pleasure outside my usual mind and body, yet thoroughly *in* them. My experience of hypnosis bears no resemblance to the common notion of a deep sleep in which the subject surrenders judgment to the hypnotist. My states are more closely related to the kind of half-sleep we enjoy in a catnap—telling ourselves we're awake and in fact hearing the clock tick or a friend in the kitchen but drifting by the moment into a welcoming harbor, the peace of which can endure for hours after returning to the world.

When I returned to normal a few minutes later, I was startled to find my three-year pain diminished by more than half. Better still, the relief lasted for the three hours Logue had estimated. The sensation was so powerful that I felt as if I'd whiffed a potent drug; I was even disturbed by the newness. But as I worked at home with a tape of Logue's voice, the strangeness passed. And in the next month, we met weekly and worked with the same methods and good new images to speed my entry on a calm acceptance of benign suggestion and the distancing of pain. Then we turned to the business of weaning me, first from the doctor's presence, then his recorded voice. The goal was that I relax myself, in my office or a crowded airport lobby, with only the trained ability to shut out distractions and return myself to a state in which I could again convince my mind to discontinue its alarm and grief at a past physical assault it could no longer warn against or repair.

One can say without fear of contradiction that Reynolds Price was an ideal candidate to reap the benefits of self-hypnosis. First of all, he experienced no apprehension about relinquishing control to the therapist (and, in fact, he remained in control of himself); but perhaps most important of all, *as a professional writer he had been using self-hypnosis for years without calling it by name.* He understood that trance could promote what psychologist Julian Rotter has described as an "internal locus of control"; that state in which we develop an expectancy that future behavior will be rewarded and a belief that we control our lives and are the "captains of our fate." Price learned to control his pain and, at the same time, began writing again after a long hiatus. He was indeed captain of his fate.

Hypnotic uncovering techniques, such as projection through the use of mental screens, can be used with less susceptible individuals. The patient is asked to imagine that he is looking at a movie or TV screen and to project onto that screen a memory from the past. The projection stimulates memory, as shown in the Spiegels' text *Trance and Treatment:*

> E.J. was a 50-year-old married mother of four, who had assumed responsibility for her brother's financial affairs during his service in the Korean War. Several years later her brother was audited by the Internal Revenue Service and the sum of ten thousand dollars was unaccounted for. Accountants had been unable to solve the mystery, and the IRS was pressing charges of tax fraud. With the trial date set for a Monday, she desperately sought help with hypnosis on the preceding Thursday.
>
> Her Profile was a one to two, and . . . she was initially disappointed that she was not capable of regression and dramatic recall, but she was taught to use the screen technique. She was instructed to try to sensitize herself to marginal thoughts and

memories on the screen, and to be especially alert to any dreams that might occur. She volunteered to have a pencil and paper near her bed. Thus an effort was made to mobilize all of her conscious and unconscious resources. On Saturday morning at breakfast her husband asked her if she had remembered anything. With disappointment, she replied that she had not. She then related a dream she had that night. In the course of the dream, she referred to a 'Jack Miller' several times. Her husband asked, 'Who the hell is Jack Miller?' She then recalled that he was a teller at a bank that she had used to handle her brother's affairs. She finally located him by phone the next day. He was now the vice-president of a Midwestern bank. She said to him, 'I feel a little silly, but I feel I need to talk to you. Do you remember me?' He replied, 'Weren't you the lady who took care of your brother's business when he was in Korea? As I recall, the last time we met I sold you several thousand dollars' worth of Series E savings bonds!' The mystery was solved, and the IRS dropped the charges.

Reexperiencing, however, is not helpful to the patient under all conditions and may be dangerous if forced. The hypnotist must act in a totally professional manner. I learned this lesson in a rather dramatic fashion when I was in my mid-twenties and attended a social weekend in the country. There were a number of guests in the group who had immigrated from Germany during the 1930s and 40s. As part of the entertainment, a stage hypnotist performed. He selected a woman from the audience who was in her late teens; she was responsive, a prize hypnotic subject. As part of the hypnosis, he took her through age regression. He said to her, "You are 15 and you're at a party with friends having a wonderful time." She floated around on stage, smiling, totally immersed in being 15. Next he said to her, "You are now five years old." Suddenly she froze; then collapsed. It turned out that she had been imprisoned in the Auschwitz concentration camp as a small child, and his suggestion was literally pulling her back into the experience. At the crucial moment all of her natural defenses came into play; her psyche protected her by taking her from the trance into a faint.

The stage hypnotist had acted irresponsibly. He was not trained or prepared to deal with problems that might rise to the surface in hypnotic exploration. He took her through age regression without knowing what was buried within her, and led her to frontiers of experience she was not prepared to reexplore. Knowing nothing about her, he had taken reckless chances in order to look good as an entertainer. As a macho hypnotist he was bent on demonstrating control over her. At the same time, he was heightening for her the power to recall memories, many of which had been long buried. Fainting was the young concentration-camp victim's way of escaping from the receptive trance state. A physician was brought in, but for three hours she could not be revived. Eventually, she dropped off to sleep, and because both fainting and sleep are nonhypnotic states, she was able to distance herself from her terrible memories.

Her case, by the way, is a perfect example of dual awareness. Her adult self knew where she was, while another part of her—her five-year-old self reexperiencing a painful memory—had no way of knowing. Because the experience proved to be unbearable, she found resources within herself that protected her.

In one of his lecture demostrations, Herbert Spiegel once presented a grade Five individual before 150 psychologists and physicians. Grade Fives are the most highly hypnotizable subjects and are measured through a special supplementary HIP testing procedure. They comprise no more than perhaps five percent of the population. He brought a man on stage who was about my own age and asked him questions while he was in the trance state. Spiegel had known the person for many years; they had a well-established, trusting relationship. Spiegel said, "It's your fifteenth birthday," and proceeded to ask questions such as "Who is the President?," and "which team won the World Series?" Because I was the same age, it was easy enough to verify the patient's answers. Spiegel then told him, "You are now four months old." The subject sucked on a pen that was offered to him. But when Spiegel said, "It's your twenty-first birthday— what year is it?" The subject for the first time came up with the wrong date. For all the other birthdays—15, 20, and the rest—he gave the correct date. We continued to question him, and he related different experiences from years surrounding his twenty-first year but nothing from that year itself.

Clearly something unpleasant had happened to the subject on his twenty-first birthday. Equally clearly, he was not prepared to share it with the audience. Even though he was in a trance, he had not totally lost the sense of where he was and what he felt a need to avoid. Spiegel was aware of what had happened, so it was not Spiegel with whom he was unwilling to share the experience but the rest of us, a group of strangers. Consummate professional that he is, Spiegel acted responsibly and made no effort to violate the subject's defenses to get him to publicly present painful memories. But Spiegel had demonstrated an important point: Even in a deep state of trance the patient can impose his own controls.

The fact is, people often forget what they are not prepared to deal with. We know that the hypnotic experience can stir up memories through the normal course of free association, and, indeed, this can be one of its uses in a therapeutic or diagnostic session. Sometimes, the patient will remember after he comes out of trance, and the resurfaced memory enables him to deal with a problem or situation in a new light. Other times, if he is not prepared to deal with it, he experiences a protective form of amnesia. Often, some six to 10 weeks later, the patient, on his own, remembers what was uncovered during trance. In any event, it is the *patient, not the therapist,* who chooses when to remember, when, if ever, he wants to deal with the material.

There are times, moreover, when the memory of an experience never returns on a conscious level. I once worked with a murderer who had absolutely no recollection of having killed his brother. He had carried out the deed in a greatly agitated state and was completely amnesic with regard to the event. I was called in by the defendant's attorneys, hypnotized him and helped him reconstruct from memory the events of that fateful day. Under hypnosis, he became progressively more worked up and excited, he recalled progressively more—the memories tumbling out while his excitement built to a crescendo leading up to the shooting—but the curious feature of the case was that the material covered under hypnosis never became consciously available to him in his waking state, and he denied that he committed the murder.

Often, issues of control emerge during the HIP evaluation. Toward the conclusion of one evaluation, I

asked my young patient, Chet, "Did you feel any lightness or floating in places other than your arm? Did
you feel lightness or floating in your body?" Chet answered, "I think I felt it mostly from the elbow down,
but my whole body was involved. But I haven't been
completely relaxed . . . When I sat down I guess I was
scared of letting my control be in somebody else's
hands. I've always had a fear of losing control. That's
why I hate drugs . . . I'm afraid of putting my control
in the hands of a foreign substance. Maybe I was afraid
I would lose myself completely—that I would go into
a dark room I couldn't escape from. The door would
close, and I would be trapped inside. I'd be swallowed
up. . . ."

In my experience, human beings fear loss of control even more than death. Most of our actions, no
matter how destructive they may be to ourselves or
others, are committed to provide us with a sense of
control. Dutch psychologist Nico H. Frijda explains
that the need for control is an emotional response to
the frightening cascade of feelings when associations
and intensity build. Often patients have said to me, "I
will never become involved with another person because I don't want to be vulnerable and get hurt ever
again." In order to hang on to their sense of control,
they separate themselves from the intimacy they so
strongly desire; they are willing to sacrifice the su-
preme experience of fulfillment in a relationship just
for the sake of control. The purpose of self-hypnosis is
not to invalidate the need for a sense of control; we all
want to control as much of our world as we can.
Rather, it is to help the patient recognize that it is
possible to act in ways that fulfill our needs—nondes-
tructive ways—without losing control. The patient
who lives in a prison in order to protect himself from

the outside world eventually discovers that prisons are not wonderful places. They offer protection at a high psychological cost.

The importance of control was demonstrated to me by a patient early in my practice. Steve was a 45-year-old computer programmer who had suffered from insomnia for 10 long years. He was desperate to find a way to sleep—medication didn't seem to help. Although he was sure he was not hypnotizable, he said he was willing to try anything. A prior patient had recommended me.

When I started to use the HIP to evaluate his hypnotic capacity, I observed that his eyeroll score was a four; a predictor that Steve was a "high". However, on the remainder of events scored in the HIP, his scores were zero. As I often do when the first approach does not provide a clear indication, I used a second induction technique—reverse hand levitation—which I learned from the psychiatrist Paul Sacerdote. In this approach, the hypnotherapist places the subject's hand in an upright position, with the elbow bent. The subject is asked to focus on a single spot on the hand, trying to recapture the image in his memory as if he were an artist or a sculptor. The patient is told that if the hand begins to feel heavy and wants to float down, permit it to do so, but slowly. If the hand feels lighter and prefers to move upward, that is also perfectly fine. Furthermore, the subject can choose to leave the hand just where it is—it makes no difference. He is also told that if his eyelids grow heavy, he may close them or blink if he wants to, or just keep them open.

Steve was clearly determined not to close his eyes or to move the hand. For 10 minutes he concentrated solely on staying absolutely still. He was intent on proving I did not have any power. I knew that already. What Steve did not know is that focused concentration is the doorway to trance. At the end of 10 minutes, all I had to do was touch Steve's hand and slowly move it downward. He immediately entered a very deep trance, and just as rapidly jumped out of the chair and out of the trance.

In the discussion that followed, I pointed out his high capacity for trance, and the fears he had of letting go of and giving up control. I proposed that at the base of his insomnia was his fear of letting go. Steve agreed completely. I told him I could teach him to do self-hypnosis, so that the control would remain with him. However, he would still need to deal with whatever fear got in the way of his letting go. I proposed that he think about what had happened in the session, and call if he wanted to pursue the issue. I am sad to say Steve never called.

The young patient, Chet, who feared that he would be trapped, had a high eye-roll, and generally high responses—although not initially. His hand, as we began, moved upwards in fits and spasms. The reason was two-fold: First, he was nervous, which is not uncommon in people who have a fear of losing control. But more importantly, he was watching himself watching me. He was the victim of his hidden observer. He could not let go and float or be free.

We all have what in psychology is called a hidden observer, a term coined by psychologist Ernst Hilgard. According to Hilgard, our hidden observer is a function of the ego—that part of us that maintains awareness of reality. In the case of Spiegel's patient who couldn't recall his twenty-first birthday, we can see the hidden observer at work: No matter how deep the trance or how regressed the patient's ego, the hidden observer remains aware and protects the patient from harm.

The following two descriptions of how the hidden observer works are from patients of Hilgard's:

The hidden observer seemed like my real self when I'm out of hypnosis, only more objective. When I'm in hypnosis, I'm imagining, letting myself pretend, but somewhere the hidden observer knows what's really going on. I think this is part of the same process as the tendency in hypnosis to stand back and say: Look what's happening to you. You're slowly going under hypnosis.

The hidden part doesn't deal with pain, it looks at what is, and doesn't judge it. It's not a hypnotized part of the self. It knows all the parts.

In the course of working with patients in hypnosis, I find that the more one observes the process, the less letting go there is likely to be. To help people let go more effectively, I attempt to merge the individual and his hidden observer using techniques that bring the hidden observer into the state of trance along with the subject.

One method is to get patients to imagine they are standing at the top of a tall staircase, looking down. The staircase is wide, with a hand rail, and they and I walk down the staircase together, taking only a single step for each number that I count. I ask them to nod when they are prepared to take the first step, and then I start to count. One: take the first step, a step down to a higher level of inner awareness. Two: the next step. Three: the next. On the tenth step, I tell them we are halfway down. I ask them to look back at the top of the staircase and nod if their observer is watching our descent. I then tell them to count their observer down to the tenth step. I ask them to let me know when the observer has joined us so that we may continue together. I then continue the count until we reach 20 and have arrived at our destination.

By integrating our hidden observer, we permit ourselves to deal more effectively with such habits and addictions as smoking, overeating, hair-pulling, and the fear of physical contact—nonmedical situations that we will examine in the next chapter. If the patient can stop "watching himself watch me, the therapist," he rids himself of extreme and inhibiting self-consciousness and can begin to participate actively in effecting change.

Chapter 4

CHOICE MAKING:

The Urge vs. the Act

HABITS OR addictions have three elements: The first is the *urge;* the second consists of the *beliefs* that support the urge; the third is the *act* itself. Most of us assume it is the urge that gets us into trouble; we seldom acknowledge the belief—the magical power—we give to the addictive act. However, the truth is that no matter how strong the urge or what the magical belief is, we can choose whether or not to act on the urge. Once we are habituated, the *only* thing we can do immediately and directly control is the act itself.

The self-hypnosis approach I use focuses primarily on choice as the method of change. A smoker, for example, has two choices—to smoke or not to smoke. The exercise that helps the patient to stop smoking also fosters a new belief system that therapeutically supports change. In what I call macho hypnosis, however, the therapist attempts to impose a belief or image on the patient. For example, he may tell you that cigarettes taste like rubber, and if you incorporate that image within you, you'll accept it for a period of time. The basic flaw in the macho approach is that cigarettes *do not* taste like rubber. The image, then, is a lie with which you comply, and lies have a short success span and generally break down.

My therapeutic approach is never to impose. I hold the view that change belongs to you, the patient, not to me, and that the way you respond to the urge to smoke is a choice—*your* choice. In life, we spend a lot of time making choices. We choose whether or not we want to express our feelings. We get angry at someone, and we choose whether or not to act out that anger by silence or by yelling, or by turning away, hurling insults, or actually fighting. We may get the urge to murder someone. Thankfully, we usually choose not to go along with that urge. We choose to act in a civilized manner. We have many urges—urges to laugh, to flirt, to escape our family responsibilities, to change jobs, to terminate a long-standing friendship, or to start a new one. We make choices as to which of these urges we will support.

Sometimes, however, we are not completely aware of our reactions. Our urges operate on a subterranean level and our choices are not conscious. Our bodies are acting for us. We have an in-born ability to communicate with our bodies, an ability we can use for good or ill. People can skip meals, gorge, or go without sleep for long periods of time because they are able to knock out the signal system that says the body needs sleep or food—or, in some cases, *does not* need food. This is a destructive use of the communications system. Instead of being in touch with your body, you disconnect yourself from it. You are denying the body's response, and the body has to complain louder and louder.

An example of how *not* doing something is a choice is demonstrated by the many people who come to me with back problems and have made no changes in the way they deal with stress. They are suffering intense pain through the neck, shoulders, and lower back. Usually these patients have lived with too much tension for too long a period of time, without any respite for the body. As a result, they have literally injured their muscles. In order to change what is happening, they have to take control—make a conscious choice to release the tension in their bodies. This may not be the final solution to their problem, but it is a step forward.

Often, we make many automatic choices that work against our own best interests. As I showed earlier in the discussion about preparation for surgery, natural is not necessarily healthy. Normally our bodies tense up when we are injured. This can be protective or harmful, depending on the nature of the injury. The very act of tensing up inhibits the flow of blood to an injured area. So, if the injury is an open wound, this is useful. However, if the injury is a strained back or a muscle pull and the body tenses to avoid pain, this inhibits the blood flow and is harmful. Blood brings all of the healing properties to injured muscles and tissues. By tensing up and lessening the flow of blood, we inhibit healing. Using self-hypnosis, we can release muscle tension, encourage the flow of blood to the injured area, and reduce the level of pain while we promote healing: We can help our bodies heal.

Since self-hypnosis promotes communication between mind and body, it can also be used to encourage love and respect for the self. When I suggest to patients that they treat themselves in a loving, respectful, and protective way, sometimes tears come to their eyes. Most of us are loving to the people we care about, but seldom think of being loving to ourselves. When you take smoke into your lungs, when you overeat, when you attack or punish yourself in any way, you are being disrespectful and destructive of self. It is sad and wasteful when people ignore the best interests of their own bodies and minds. It seems to be very difficult for us to view ourselves in such a considerate light. When such knowledge comes, it comes as a shock. Of all the work I do in therapy, nothing is more important than this message: Without healthy self-love, self-respect, and understanding, there can be no change.

When a patient comes to see me who wants to stop smoking, I start by asking the patient how much he smokes, how long he's been smoking and why he wants to stop at this time. In our initial contact, I'm not only trying to learn about the patient's smoking experience, but also to understand the patient. Because the patient is new to me, I can't assume his request is simply a healthy attempt to deal with a problem. On rare occasions, patients who seek help for what appears to be a simple problem are on the verge of a serious psychological breakdown. The approach to these patients obviously needs to be different.

When I feel comfortable about moving ahead, I then ask three very key questions: At what age did you start? What did you think smoking would do for you? What do you think smoking does for you now? The age of initiation is an important question in predicting the likelihood of success or failure of treatment. It is known that the later in life you start, the easier it seems to be to stop. The belief system that supports smoking tends to be more primitive and ingrained among those who start in their early teens.

When Paul came to me, he was a 33-year-old actor-singer, a heavy smoker with a long-time habit. He had managed to stop smoking a number of times for a matter of weeks or months, but had always gone back.

"How old were you when you began smoking ciga-rettes?"

"Twelve, thirteen. Somewhere in there," he replied. "I can't remember exactly."

"Can you tell me what you thought smoking would do for you?" I asked.

He grinned. "Make me a big man! I mean not just in the eyes of others—girls, other guys—but to myself. You know, a Bogart, a John Wayne. Paul the real man." He looked down and shook his head. "I guess that's stupid, isn't it? I was just another stupid kid trying to grow up too fast."

The questions I asked Paul were designed to seek out a belief system that supported his smoking habit, and to understand and challenge it. Paul soon began to understand that we give our addictions magical power over us.

"I can't sit around relaxing with friends if I don't have a cigarette," he said with wonder. "I can't drink a cup of coffee without a cigarette, or have a beer without one. Everything I've been doing with my life seems tied up with smoking. I mean *everything*. Eating, sing-ing, acting, talking, worrying, making love, you name it. Everything's punctuated with smoke. It's almost as though cigarettes do the drinking and help me to get up for rehearsals."

When I feel I understand the patient well enough to prepare an individualized self-hypnosis exercise, I ask about previous experience with hypnosis and, espe-cially if there is none, what he feels about hypnosis. I then evaluate the patient's hypnotic capacity. When the HIP test is complete and I tell the patient where he is on the hypnotic capacity scale, I then teach him a self-hypnosis exercise—a technique that will reinforce his desire to choose not to smoke, challenge the belief system that supports the urge, and offer strategies for dealing with the urge.

This is what I often tell my patients:

"Relax and think about the things I'm going to say. Smoking poisons your body. It destroys lung tissue. It clogs the cardiovascular system. It irritates the throat.

"We often forget that we need our bodies to live. Much of what we are able to do, many of the pleasures we experience, the excitement and joy, are messages that have arrived through our bodies. I'm going to repeat: We need our bodies to live, we and our bodies are one. Because you need your body to live, you owe your body protection. By protecting your body, you show love and respect for yourself." Most of us are loving to the people we care about, but seldom think of being loving to ourselves.

"You smoke two packs of cigarettes a day. I'm going to suggest something to you that at first may sound radical, but in fact the more you think about it, the more sensible it's going to become. One of the ways you can protect your body and show respect for yourself is by responding to the urge to smoke by *choosing* not to smoke. This is not a battle between you and yourself. Believe me, any battle you have with yourself you are bound to lose."

We know from research that if you choose not to smoke, the urge itself will diminish. I suggest to my nicotine-habituated patients that they can treat themselves respectfully by choosing not to smoke. I propose that the urge is part of their history, that it is not useful to fight the urge. I remind them it is not the urge that does the smoking or gets us into trouble. If that were true, we would *all* be in trouble. It is the act of smoking we have to conquer, not the urge.

We know that people practice celibacy for a number of reasons. Sex is a strong urge and yet people can choose to be celibate. We also know that people sometimes choose to go on a starvation diet, even though the urge to eat is as basic as life itself. We know that each time you choose not to go along with an urge, it becomes easier the next time to bypass it, and over time the urge occurs less and less often. I tell my patients that even though I haven't smoked for 12 years, there is still an occasional urge to smoke. I know what my choice is, however, and I choose not to smoke. I ask them to imagine themselves choosing not to smoke and feeling pleased each time they choose not to go along with the urge. Each time you choose not to smoke, you reinforce your own commitment to be protective of your body, and loving and respectful of yourself.

The self-hypnosis exercise I taught Paul, the actor, was to imagine he was waiting for an audition for a very important role. It was a role in a musical, created and produced by people he respected, and he would be given a major acting and singing part. As he thought about smoking while he waited, he realized his throat would become raspy. He could choose between smoking or performing at his optimum. Even though he had the urge to smoke, the act was still a matter of choice, his choice. He was to visualize himself choosing his performance, not the cigarette, and being pleased with the choice he made.

At this point in my sessions, I then pause for a moment or two to give the patient time to think about all the things I've said. I remind the patient, if it fits his case, that he started smoking as an adolescent because he felt the cigarette made him look more sophisticated. Now he has become that sophisticated person and he no longer needs the cigarette to bolster that image, which in fact has become a reality.

We sit in silence then. The patient is in a state of trance, and I often enter into a similar state of trance because I am so focused on the exercise. I ask the patient to think about his own personal reasons for treating himself in a loving and protective manner by choosing not to smoke. After a moment I bring the patient out of trance. I tell him "I'm going to count backwards from three to one. At three, I want you to get ready. At two, with your eyes still closed, I want you to look up. And, at one, open your eyes and let them slowly come into focus." I then count three . . . two . . . one and that's the end of the exercise.

So the hypnotic exercise is really composed of the following: You, the patient, enter the trance state—which is simply a heightened state of communication—where you imagine the way you want to behave, using visual, sensual, and visceral imagery. Then you give yourself the message that you and your body will work together to protect it from injury by *choosing* not to smoke. You remind yourself that the *act* is a choice. Then, you exit from trance slowly and easily by counting backwards from three to one.

Afterwards, I repeat many of the issues I discussed in trance. I want to help the patient understand that he often gives cigarettes a kind of magical power. Although he may feel that smoking enhances his manhood or solves his problems, it is he—not the cigarette—who acts like a man and solves problems.

I tell him about the salesmen who come to me to stop smoking and, at the time, truly believe they can't call on an account or close without a cigarette. I describe the writers who tell me they can't write without smoking. They speak as if the cigarettes are doing the writing. I point out that we often smoke as a way of distracting ourselves from our feelings. That when we use cigarettes for distraction, we rob ourselves of potential richness in our lives. Writers who stop smoking often find that their writing improves; they report they are now more in touch with the feelings and experiences from which their writing derives.

What does the habituated smoker learn in hypnosis? He learns that smoking is a choice he makes in response to the urge. *But the urge is not a choice.* Feelings, desires, beliefs, and urges are not choices. The urges are automatic, integrated into the human system. But the action he takes in response to the urge is a choice. He can choose what his actions are. The patient is encouraged to ask questions and be free to express emotion. Sometimes there are tears. Sometimes a feeling of overpowering relief.

For the first week following our session, I ask my smoking patients to do the exercise anywhere from 8 to 10 times a day. I point out that the exercise takes only 90 seconds and they can't overdose on it. I teach them a way to do the exercise privately, and a way they can do it in public—even at a cocktail or dinner party. "Am I doing it correctly?" is a common question I get from patients. "Did I go deep enough?" Luckily, for therapeutic purposes, depth of trance has no meaning. The awareness of the external world will vary from time to time. As is the case when learning any skill, repetition is the key to success. The more the self-hypnosis exercise is done, the more effective it becomes. You, the patient, continue to do the exercise until you know you are committed not to smoke. For some people, two to three times a day over a period of several weeks is effective; others need to do the exercise more frequently and for longer periods.

Eating can prove to be a much more complex problem than smoking, as the case of Martha clearly illustrates. When she first came to me she was an attractive woman who weighed about 50 pounds more than she should. She had been in analysis for years and complained that it didn't seem to help. "I'm spending all this money to get rid of excess pounds," she told me, "and my analyst says my weight is only part of the problem. He says I've got things in my background that are making me eat. But I want to deal with my weight problem; I'm not interested in my childhood. I haven't got years to do this. It's the money, for one thing. My husband's insurance doesn't cover therapy."

I understood her impatience. From her point of view, the analyst was refusing to deal immediately with what *she* considered the pressing problem at hand, and, instead insisted on reviewing her history and delving into her unconscious. I explained that in self-hypnosis we focus on the specific problem, which we are often able to resolve without thoroughly exploring underlying issues. Often an analysis can become bogged down in what appears to be an unsolvable problem—such as weight control—and dealing directly with the issue via hypnosis helps to alleviate the therapeutic roadblock. However, I went on, that didn't rule out the usefulness of the analytic method; it depends on the nature of the overall problem. In many cases, self-hypnosis is used as an adjunct to psychoanalysis. I have often used it with my own analytic patients, and with those referred to me by other analysts.

As in any form of therapy, I started by taking Martha's history. She grew up in the midwest, the daughter of a successful plumbing-supply manufacturer. She had an older brother, a brilliant boy doted on by his parents, who graduated from college before his twentieth birthday and is now an economics professor at a prestigious eastern university. From as early as she could remember, Martha was type-cast as the "cuddly" one, the "toy child" of the family. "I remember how happy and amused my family was by my large appetite," she said. "At family gatherings— Thanksgiving and Christmas—I got attention and praise for eating extra helpings of food. It was considered 'cute.' It was a way of taking the spotlight away from my brother, with his precocious vocabulary and ideas."

Weight was a constant problem, from pre-puberty on. She could not remember how many times in her life she had dieted, then binged with a vengeance. "I've tried about every diet known to man," she told me. "Scarsdale, Beverly Hills, Drinking Man, Water Retention, Papaya, and on and on. They all seem to hold out promise at first, but none of them work. Nothing changes in the place in me where I crave food."

Martha's problem became complicated by a recent second marriage (her first, childless marriage ended in divorce). Her husband, as she puts it, is "slim and handsome. He feels I'll be much more beautiful if I lose weight, and he'll be more 'proud' of me. He uses the word 'proud' which upsets me. I say to him, 'Why aren't you proud of me for who I am, not how much I weigh?' But I understand his position. His work involves a lot of socializing and he wants me to be a part of that. But when I binge and gain more weight, we get in these awful arguments."

I started by explaining to Martha that because

food is necessary, the urge to eat can truly be a healthy, normal response to the body's need for nourishment. Nonetheless, we can lose weight and prevent weight gain in a way that will let us feel positive about our bodies. In her case, eating too much had its root in winning the love of others. Her family encouraged her to eat, and unconsciously she continued to believe that by eating she could win the love and attention she strongly desired. She learned, however—at least intellectually—that eating to earn love and attention doesn't work. I started by pointing out some things she already knew; by overeating she was actually being very self-destructive. First of all, she was angry at herself for being out of control and putting on weight; second, she could no longer use eating to take the spotlight away from her brother. The attention she received was exactly the opposite of what she wanted.

Martha was a grade One on the HIP scale for hypnotic capacity, which is at the extreme low end of the scale, but fortunately, she was fully motivated. I put her into trance and asked her to imagine a large screen with two sections. On the left half of the screen she could see herself as she was right now, with much more weight than she wanted to carry. I talked to Martha about realistic weight-loss goals. I urged her to consider that losing one or two pounds a week would be a powerful accomplishment. I suggested that she see herself losing 10 to 15 pounds over a three-month period. I asked her to fix clearly in her mind how she looked, either in a state of dress or undress.

On the right half of the screen, I asked her to see herself as she would like to look and feel three months from now. I suggested that she might remember how she looked 10 years ago, perhaps wearing a particular style of clothing she yearned to wear if she were only thinner.

Once having fixed her present and future images on the two-paneled screen, I told her she was looking into a magic screen. She could twist a knob and transform the left part of the screen into the right part of the screen—she could transform herself as she was now into the physical person she wanted to be. I then outlined some of the ways she could make that magic a reality.

While she was in a trance, part of her exercise was to imagine herself being very selective each time she had the urge to eat. She would focus on the one or two foods she most desired. There would be no more need —once she was focused, centered—to go to the kitchen and simply eat her way through the refrigerator. If she realized she truly wanted some chocolate ice cream, then she should *have* chocolate ice cream, even if it meant getting dressed and walking a few blocks to the neighborhood confectionary for the thing she craved. The first step in treating herself lovingly and respectfully was to make every effort to eat what she really wanted to eat rather than simply stuffing herself.

Now I asked her to imagine going to the store for the ice cream and bringing it home. She put a scoop in a dish. I told her that she had a desire for this special texture and taste, and now was the chance to derive all the pleasure, all the sensation from it that she could. After swallowing the first spoonful and before taking another, I asked her to ask herself whether she wanted any more of that taste and texture. If the answer was yes, then she should again take a small amount, place it in her mouth and savor it, and continue to eat it in that way until she found she was satisfied. If the answer was no, then no matter how little or how much was left, she should stop eating.

Out of trance, Martha told me that one part of the exercise bothered her. "It's true I love chocolate ice cream. But should I be using the exercise this way? I mean, how can it help me? Ice cream is fattening."

I told her not to worry if she sometimes craved chocolate ice cream instead of a stalk of celery. "If you choose only what's good for you, you'll set up a deprivation syndrome, and then when you stop dieting you'll gain the weight right back. The goal of the exercise is to get you to satisfy your hunger without overeating, and yet to eat what you enjoy. If you wait for the full-stomach syndrome, you're in trouble." I explained that it takes 20 minutes for the "my stomach is full" signal to reach the brain, and if you're eating rapidly, which most people who gain weight do, you can consume a tremendous amount of food after your stomach is full and before the signal reaches you. Look around in any restaurant and notice how quickly overweight people devour food; they hardly seem aware of what they eat.

Obviously, food is necessary even for those overweight, and some of the time the urge to eat is truly a healthy, normal response to the body's need for nourishment. A useful approach is to find a variety of foods you like and that are good for you. Diets are a perfect time for discovering new meals and snacks. I approach the problem by showing you that you can lose weight in a way that will let you feel positive about yourself. If you eat too much, it is often because in our society eating is a way of being loving toward ourselves. It is a reminder of parental love in which the presentation of food is a loving act. The rest of the world may kick you in the teeth, but food is a way you can be nice to yourself.

I prescribed that Martha do a self-hypnosis exercise about eight times a day—approximately once every two hours, for 90 seconds. The exercise was to first see herself on two screens: the way she looked at the present and the way she would like to look. Then, she was to imagine herself selecting what she wanted to eat, and savoring the special tastes and textures. Finally, she was to see herself stop eating when she was no longer enjoying the food, no matter how little or how much was left. As part of the prescription, I asked her to look in the mirror each morning, preferably with a minimal amount of clothing, so that she could project in the exercise an accurate view of the way she looked then. And as I do with all weight-control patients, I asked her to call me in a week. At first the exercise proved difficult, because when people have gained weight they tend to avoid looking at themselves in the mirror as a way to avoid dealing with the problem. Later, it became easier, and finally, as Martha continued to lose weight, a pleasure.

When weight-control patients ask to see me a second time after the initial visit and phone reinforcement, I ask how often they have done the exercise. I make it clear to them, as I do with my smoking patients, that the exercise has absolutely no downside risks. You cannot overdose on it.

In the first week, they should do their exercise as prescribed—at least eight to 10 times a day. Sometimes a patient will tell me, "I've been busy. I only had time to do it two or three times." "How come?" I ask. "Here you have a technique that has a good chance of helping you lose weight. Why aren't you using it?" I've found that many people use weight as a shield, just as Martha did. It is not food they want so much as a shield against the complexities of life.

As University of Pittsburgh psychologists Carlos H. Grillo, Saul Shiffman, and Rena R. Wing found in a study of the coping skills of dieters, the better equipped they were with a technique to handle emotional upset and anger, the less likely they were to relapse. The self-hypnosis approach I use provides a way in which dieters can focus on their goals and support their efforts, while acknowledging the situations that make them angry or upset.

I suggest to my weight patients that they begin to take charge of their bodies. Reducing the amount of food one takes in is not sufficient to maintain a weight loss. To lose and then keep weight at a desirable level, one must also exercise as a way to keep in shape and burn off some of the calories consumed. I believe that for people to reach certain goals and to feel good about themselves in the process, vigorous physical activity in keeping with age and condition (walking and swimming are ideal forms of exercise) can be as important as mental activity.

The last time I heard from Martha, five months after our first and only session, her voice radiated happiness. "I love to look in the mirror now. I've lost 33 pounds," she said. "Seventeen to go, but I know I'll make it, though I don't use chocolate ice cream in my exercise any more. I'm sick of it. I've switched to rice pudding."

Alcohol is a much more difficult addiction to handle than either smoking or eating. By the time people come to see me, most have already lost their desire and motivation to change—and motivation is the key element in change. Alcohol, like long-term drug behavior (more often than not, these days, cocaine and heroin use), tends to make people amotivational. As psychiatrist Edward J. Khantzian, a specialist on drug treatment programs, has pointed out, addictive behavior starts as a form of self-medication. He argues that the major difficulty in treating recreational drug users is that their ability to take care of themselves is severely impaired. They have no sense of danger or concern, despite obvious deterioration. Their motivation to choose and act differently is severely diminished.

Without the desire to succeed, the techniques I use seldom work. The majority of alcoholics come to me because someone has insisted they come, not because they want to change. I work with them, but I tell them that the exercise is not likely to help unless they join a support group like Alcoholics Anonymous (AA) to keep them on track. While AA does not work for everyone, when an individual is ambivalent about change group support is a necessity along with professional treatment.

If, on the other hand the motivation is clearly there, it is possible that self-hypnosis will be very effective. The patient has a good reason to stop drinking.

Beth came to me in the second month of pregnancy. Her obstetrician had warned her that wine before and with dinner (she and her husband were habitués of the "cocktail hour") could possibly damage a fetus. Although Beth was by no means an out-of-control alcoholic, she had developed a habit over the years that had become entrenched. She was clearly unhappy without her daily two glasses of Chablis.

I created a self-hypnotic exercise for Beth in which she imagined her baby had been born and she was sitting next to the child softly singing her to sleep. She went on to imagine that later in the evening she and her husband sat together in the living room, holding hands, happily making plans for a trip with the baby. Beth did this exercise faithfully, twice a day, and it worked. She gave up wine with no regrets.

Again, you can learn the self-hypnosis technique, you can learn how to use it, but you must *choose* to use it. You are being offered a choice—a most powerful choice. You now have to *want* to use the technique. You have to apply it in order for it to be effective.

When Emily came to me she was in her mid-twenties and struggling to be a journalist. She had achieved a certain degree of success in college—she was a star "investigative" reporter on the weekly newspaper— and assumed that her career after college would follow a steady upward course. Instead, after moving from the midwest to New York City where she felt the opportunities were the greatest in her field, she found the competition fierce. There were many like Emily trying to break into the literary big time—either as book or magazine editors, or as successful free-lance journalists.

The first time she came to me, she was wearing a kerchief, which didn't seem appropriate to her age or style of dress. She was genuinely puzzled about her condition. In a shaky voice, she told me her history and how hard she was working trying to sell articles to newspapers or magazines. She told me how she would get upset and churn inside whenever she received a rejection slip. But worst of all, an early teen-age problem had returned—she was unconsciously pulling the hair from her head; she was ashamed that she needed to wear a kerchief. It could happen when she was reading, writing, or just watching TV.

Emily suffered from trichotillomania, a disorder in which people have an unconscious urge to pull out their hair to such a degree that some develop large bald spots. Victimized by a fear response that allowed anger to be expressed only in such a bizarre manner, Emily lived in a constant state of misery. Once her frustration and feeling of impotency built up to a certain point, her childhood illness returned. She was not aware of the excruciating pain she was inflicting on herself while it was happening; her inner-turmoil coupled with her hypnotic capacity overrode any awareness of the damage she was doing, physical or psychological. Nor had she understood the link in her case between her frustration and hair pulling.

Emily felt that her body was her enemy and she needed to fight with herself to break the habit; there was something inside her she couldn't control that made her pull out her hair. She was convinced that if she were a truly good person, she wouldn't have a problem.

I taught Emily a self-hypnosis exercise that challenged those beliefs and gave her a choice. In the exercise, she imagined how wonderful it would be when she didn't have to cover her head—how wonderful it would be to protect her body from injury. I asked her to imagine her body sending her a signal whenever her hand started to reach up to pull out her hair. I suggested that each time that feeling grew in her, she should stroke her hair in a loving way and think about how nice her hair looked and felt when it was full. I prescribed that she do her exercise for 90 seconds every two hours. Within the week, Emily gained the awareness she needed to stop the hair-pulling. Three months later, Emily's hair had grown in, and she left

New York for another city where she felt she could grow and prosper as a writer.

Jackie, an attractive, bright, 26-year-old who was working on a graduate degree in history, is an example of someone who was in treatment with a colleague, in both individual and couples therapy. Her therapist sent her to me in the hope that I could teach her how to relax. She was having problems being touched, even by her boy friend. When anyone touched her she was flooded with negative feelings that overwhelmed her.

During that first session, we talked a little. I evaluated her hypnotic capacity, which was in the mid-range, and taught her a relaxation exercise in which she was to imagine she was at the beach, lying in the sand. I told her that the sun was shining, warming her body, and she was listening to the soft, rhythmic sound of the water lapping against the shore. I watched her enter trance, her body fully relaxed. I realized however, that just getting Jackie to relax was not the end of the problem. At that point, after telling her I was going to do so, I grasped her wrist with my fingers, as I had done during the HIP test. I had noticed when I was testing her that even though my touch had been brief and obviously a professional part of the evaluation, she had tensed. And now she tensed once again.

With my hand lightly grasping her wrist, I asked Jackie to describe what she was feeling. She explained that she was overwhelmed with the same feelings she had had as a child. My touch created ambivalence: She was frightened by my touch and found it threatening, yet at the same time she had a sense of her own strong desire for warmth and support. I asked if she wanted me to remove my hand, and she replied that she wasn't sure. The session ended with Jackie visibly shaken.

In the sessions of hypnosis that followed, I first held Jackie's wrist and then her hand so that she could also hold or touch. As we worked, images of her childhood came pouring out. Jackie was the oldest child of parents who were alcoholics. She had seen many a night, starting at the age of eight, in which her parents came home falling-down drunk; she had had to undress them and put them to bed. Watching people drink, the touch of another, the sight of skin, flooded Jackie with all the images and feelings associated with that period in her life.

I worked with Jackie for about 20 sessions over a period of two years. During trance and in our sessions together, she was able to express feelings and reactions that had been long buried. She learned that she could choose to touch or be touched, as well as refuse to touch or be touched. She could say yes or no! She was able to choose for the first time!

About a month after our final session, Jackie wrote to me. "It would be far too difficult to tell you all that has happened. Just to highlight things, though, I am touching people more easily. I didn't notice it at first because it was all so spontaneous. I am actually reaching out to make contact. It's great! I still struggle with the intense feelings that come up from my early life, but at least I'm moving in a good direction."

As I mentioned above, Jackie was able to choose to touch or be touched; just as Martha was able to choose to eat or not to eat in an appropriate way; just as Paul learned to follow his choices and not his urges in order to quit smoking. Good choices, we have learned, empower us.

There are conditions, however, that don't lend themselves to the application of the urge-choice principle we've been discussing. We will now look at some of those cases, many of which have both physical and psychological components.

Chapter 5

DEALING WITH ILLNESS:

How Mind-Body Unity Can Often Lead to Solutions

THE CONCEPT of mind-body separation—dualism—probably arose during the earliest stages of the scientific revolution. The French mathematician and philosopher René Descartes, for example, believed that the world was divided between matter and mind. As proof of his existence, he stated in the well known phrase, "I think, therefore I am." Although it was a useful concept at the time, the retention of such strict duality as the "scientific" approach has led to the current difficulty in identifying illness or other problems as somatic (body) *or* psychological, (mind). I believe that the unity of body and mind, rather than duality, enhances our ability to diagnose and treat medical conditions.

Over the years, I have learned that it is arbitrary —and foolhardy—to set up any kind of division between mind and body, as the case of Alice so dramatically illustrates. When she was first referred to me, she was under treatment for an unknown dermatological condition. Her terrible itching attacks had started suddenly about 3 years before. She had no previous history of skin disorder, yet she had come home one afternoon and, in her own words, "The weirdest feeling came over me. I started scratching uncontrollably and finally pulled my sweater off, thinking there must be something inside it. There wasn't, but I noticed my body was covered with a very fine rash and was extremely itchy."

Her physician could find no physical basis for her condition, and none of the medication prescribed alleviated the problem enough for her to function either socially or professionally. Alice went to a number of dermatologists, and hospitals, forever being tested, always searching for a cure. Nothing worked; she was in great despair and even greater discomfort. In an account describing her terrifying medical saga which she later wrote and gave to me, she stated:

Things continued to get worse. I started losing weight and more ailments accompanied the rash that seemed to be jumping all over my body. I tried very hard to continue a normal life, at home and on the job. During this period I developed iritus, bursitus in both shoulders and a paralyzing pain from my neck to my knees that made it almost impossible for me to dress myself. The pain never completely disappeared and would wake me at night out of a light sleep. I felt that some monster had taken over my body. At the same time I was being tested for various diseases. The doctors took blood out of me and pumped drugs into me. My skin was on fire and looked as though it had turned to dust. On my worst days I would scream with pain and frustration. I started losing my hair.

More drugs, more biopsies, sleeping pills and anti-histamines. I began to lose track of time. I hallucinated. When I looked into a mirror and saw this scarecrow of a woman with no hair and skin that was a mixture of red blotches and pale dust, I had no idea who it was.

My doctor was totally frustrated. He searched for clues in my homelife. Was my marriage okay? Was I having problems with my children? Any problems I had at home had been going on for years and I felt I had found ways of handling them. I had taken on enormous responsibilities, the work was good therapy. My children were supportive and caring. Home was not the answer for the horror I was going through.

Finally, the resident in charge of Alice's case during a particularly lengthy hospital stay, suspecting there might be a psychological component to her problem, suggested hypnosis might be helpful. Alice's husband quickly concurred, and the case was referred to me. One of the unfortunate fallouts of the prevailing belief in the separateness of mind and body is that it makes the concept of a "psychological component" one of last resort, so that psychological intervention is often not considered until medical testing and treatment proves unsuccessful.

When I first saw Alice, she was asleep in her hospital bed, yet her eyes were wide open. Her pupils were hidden; only the white of her eyeballs were showing, in what could be labeled "the ultimate eyeroll." Here, it seemed, was someone with great hypnotic capacity. Because hypnotic intervention has been effective in the treatment of some skin disorders, I felt that self-hypnosis would probably help her. When she woke up, I did a HIP evaluation and, even though she was full of drugs that limited her ability to concentrate, she scored a four. In the required supplementary test, which I did later, she demonstrated the highest capacity, a grade Five. When she awakened and we talked about her illness, I asked her to tell me her deepest wish. She answered without a second's hesitation, "To be able to control the itching." I asked her when she felt the most relief from it. She told me that a soothing shower—the sensation of water running over her body—was the only way she could feel any comfort. I taught her to use her impressive hypnotic capacity to enter trance and to imagine she was in the shower. I suggested that she set the water at the most desirable temperature and feel the water flowing over her body. Through hypnosis, we were accessing her visceral memory; she told me later that the relief she felt almost immediately was tremendous.

Looking at her body's response, I could actually see her in the shower letting the water run over her body; I could see how it soothed her and the relief in her face as the muscles relaxed and as the water brought blessed relief from the incessant itching. I told her she could stay in the trance as long as she liked, and when she was ready she could come out and bring that feeling out with her. Her body would remember what it felt like when she was in the shower.

In a few minutes, Alice emerged from the trance but retained the feeling. I told her she could do this exercise anytime she chose, and that it would be a good idea to practice the exercise once an hour for the first week. Just as with other unfamiliar routines, practice makes you more proficient. Whenever she felt herself growing uncomfortable, she could put herself in a state of trance, which I told her was a state of communication. Hypnosis, I explained, was a way for her to let her body know how she wanted it to feel or behave. The state of hypnosis enhanced communication and permitted her to be in close touch with her body. It was a way for her to talk to her body, and also a way for her body to tell her what it was experiencing and feeling.

Although we had used self-hypnosis to alleviate a disturbing symptom, we were far from resolving her problems, or curing her illness. Her case was so complex and deeply rooted that I felt the only way to help her on a long-term basis was to try and find the source of her disturbance.

During our first session, I had taken a brief history. One important piece of information about Alice's character surfaced immediately. She needed to please everyone. No matter how busy she was at work, people at her office knew to "ask Alice" if they wanted to get something done. At home there was always too much to do in too little time. She had become nervous and chronically exhausted, and her beloved dog had become sick as well. To get a picture of her state of mind at the time, I scheduled a second appointment for the next day, and suggested we use trance to take her back in time and find out what happened during that period when her rash and itching first erupted. I explained to her that with her high capacity, she not only could go back in time, but could literally reexperience what had happened to her by accessing different forms of memory—visceral, visual, and verbal. I guided her into trance and took her back to the time just before the rash first appeared.

While in trance, she spoke in a quiet, anguished manner, and it was clear she was reexperiencing that painful period three years earlier. She talked about her dog Nipper, a 15-year-old part-Cocker Spaniel, and the rash the dog had developed. Nipper couldn't stop scratching, causing open sores and bleeding all over her body. Medication was proving useless, and finally the vet told Alice that Nipper should be put to sleep, but he left the decision to her. "I did everything I could just so she wouldn't scratch. I tried to save her —bathing her constantly, walking her, talking to her, and soothing her. She was driving my husband crazy. He said it was my fault the dog had become sick, and that the dog should be put to sleep. I began to feel it *was* my fault," Alice said. The dog got worse and finally had to be destroyed. She was the one who made the arrangements and was holding Nipper when the vet put her to sleep.

Alice's trance produced some vital information. It seemed clear that the trauma she suffered when her dog became sick and then died, along with her guilt, were the triggers for the rash she developed. Her emotional state, the fatigue, exhaustion, and stress made her vulnerable to a variety of illnesses. Somehow, her dog's scratching became her scratching. Highly hypnotizable, able to communicate with her body, it is possible that she expressed her feelings through her physical symptoms. We do not understand enough about mind-body communication to know what actually happened, but whatever occurred created changes in the cells of her skin. Her symptoms at the time that I saw her—undoubtedly exacerbated by high doses of Cortisone—represented a complex physical breakdown. A week after the self-hypnosis treatment began, Alice's low-grade fever, which she had had for months, was gone and she was soon after released from the hospital. With her skin condition alleviated, Alice was able to deal with other issues and return to a normal life.

There are times, however, when the mind-body connection does not offer a solution to a problem. In such cases, there are limits to the therapeutic value of self-hypnosis, or any other type of psychological and even physical interventions. Adam is an example of such a case.

Adam came to me complaining of a lower back problem. He had consulted a number of physicians and had had all types of treatment. The doctors had concluded that his pain was psychological—that is, that it might have resulted from stress or some other psychological phenomena. The hope was that he could use hypnosis to alleviate the stress and the pain, and perhaps uncover the source.

I taught Adam self-hypnosis and, through the use of a hypnotic exercise, he was able to reduce the pain somewhat but not eliminate it. We also explored issues in his life that might have promoted the problem, to little avail; although the intensity of the pain was somewhat reduced, it still erupted at odd moments. I felt intuitively that if the back pain was solely a psychological response, he would have shown greater improvement after a combined hypnotic and psychotherapeutic approach. I urged him to continue to seek a physical source for his problem. He had a number of additional workups and eventually it was discovered that he had pancreatic cancer. What had seemed to be a psychological problem with physical symptoms was not psychological. Although self-hypnosis—a psychological technique—helped to bring him temporary relief, the source of his pain was found to be physical after all.

Sometimes both physicians and psychologists put a psychological label on physical complaints that are not supported by diagnostic testing. Though any disorder may have roots in both mind and body, as pointed out above, we cannot assume that the lack of physical evidence is always proof of a psychological problem.

Mary's case, like Adam's, illustrates that the psychological and the physical elements of illness, which are so bound together, also need to be understood separately. A 79-year-old postoperative patient, Mary had been successfully operated on for the removal of an abdominal mass, but after her recovery she was having difficulty urinating. The doctors were puzzled; they could find no blockage or other physical reason for the problem. They therefore concluded that her difficulty had a psychological root.

Her physician sent her to see a psychiatrist who, knowing my work, referred her to me. It was impossible for Mary to function in a socially normal way, because when the need to urinate built up over a number of hours, the pain immobilized her and she had to go to a hospital to be catheterized. She was afraid to leave her home or be too far from a hospital. We used an approach most of us have long forgotten to help Mary deal with the problem. Urination is a letting go. When we urinate, we release the sphincter that closes the bladder. As children, we are toilet-trained. We learn to tighten the sphincter in order to control the flow. The focus of Mary's self-hypnosis exercise was to relax and let go. When she had to urinate, she would think of being in a very pleasant place and imagine letting all her muscles become very loose and open— she would just relax, let go, and let the urine flow.

I told Mary that once she started to urinate I wanted her to stop the stream and start again. Therapeutically, I was working to give her back her sense of control. Sometimes she had to sit on the john for an hour before the stream would flow, but through her exercise she at least reached the point where she knew she could always urinate if she relaxed and waited. She did not have to suffer the intense pain of a full bladder, nor did she have to be afraid of being far from a hospital. Thanks to her exercise and her experience, she was confident that she could control her stream.

With my support, Mary continued to push for a physical explanation of the problem. Three weeks later, the doctors found a blockage in Mary's urethra. A stone had worked its way down, blocking the flow. And so her problem was physical, not psychological in origin, and yet through self-hypnosis she had managed to relax her urethra enough to empty her bladder.

When Greta came to me she was, as she put it, in "a state of misery, pure misery." She was a retired accountant, a well-groomed and well-spoken woman with wide cultural interests and friendships. Until about a year before our first session, she had been an "up" person—always on the go, gregarious and fun-loving. She told me that it was her habit to put her entire self into every project, including refurbishing her beautiful, pre-war apartment on Manhattan's upper west side.

In her lifetime, she had never known the meaning of the word depression until the summer of 1987 when she began experiencing a number of alarming symptoms: Her skin became dry, scaly and thin; her bowel movements frequent, runny and painful; and she could not sleep. Slender to begin with, she suffered extreme weight loss. Her family physician ignored the symptoms through the fall and into the winter, giving her pills and assuring her the problem would go away. But it didn't go away. During that period her depression grew. She told me that "terrible stuff" kept running through her mind—everything was bleak and totally dark. This fundamentally optimistic woman who had always looked forward to each new day, now looked forward to nothing. Even the sunny days were shadowed. It got to the point where she couldn't talk to anyone—including close friends—without crying or screaming. Fear and terror enveloped her, physically and mentally. She was certain that she was losing her mind.

Finally, after undergoing a series of tests, it was determined that she had a serious yeast infection—her immune system had ceased to function effectively. A health-conscious woman who had always taken good care of herself, Greta had been eating brewer's yeast steadily for 15 to 20 years as a B-complex vitamin supplement to her diet. It can happen with supplements and drugs that an overdose or heavy, sustained use can have the opposite effect than that for which it was intended. It's possible that the brewer's yeast was a contributing factor.

By the time she came to me, the yeast infection was beginning to respond to the medication—but she was afraid it could resume at any minute. She was told to be very careful about what she ate. She was on a very strict diet. At times it seemed the infection had ended, but it soon returned. She was fearful of any action that would restart the illness. She explained to me that she was existing in a big black hole, which was extending into her spine and into her heart and rib area; blackness was suffocating her. In fact, death would be preferable if it meant getting rid of the pain and her terrible thoughts.

She told me she had tried psychiatry but it had been, to quote her, "a complete fiasco. The man was giving me all kinds of rules that meant nothing to me.

Empathetic he was not. He was a pill pusher. I felt I was going to have to go it alone, but I can't *do* it by myself. I'm in need of help." She continued to cry.

I could see that she felt alone and isolated from the world. I told her to imagine being in a place she had always loved, and that she was there with friends she loved. She enjoyed walking in the woods, and so I told her to imagine walking in the woods, smelling the leaves, the earth, and hearing the sounds of birds and the wind rustling in the limbs of the trees. In trance, she was there—it was clear that she was there in the woods. She saw and felt the woods and experienced a beautiful sunset. She cried, but she also began to relax.

Greta learned a self-hypnosis exercise that involved her favorite places and favorite people, and I told her to use it at home, or on the street, or driving, or anywhere—whenever she felt the depression coming on.

By our third session, her mood began to improve and she was relearning how it felt to feel good, which is never easy when you have lived through a protracted depression. Lightness was replacing heaviness and darkness. After going into trance and practicing her self-hypnosis exercise, she was more and more able to say, "That feels good!" She was learning once again to savor the good moments, to hold on to them as precious things. The more she could do that, the more quickly the bad moments evaporated. Self-hypnosis was relaxing both her body and mind. Relaxation was replacing tightness.

Greta came to me for six sessions, and then felt well enough to be on her own. She called to tell me that the yeast infection was over and her doctor had reported that her immune system responses were at normal levels. She still suffers from occasional depression, but not as deep or lasting as before. She may never be quite the sunny disposition she was before her illness, but in many ways she feels she has gained added strength: she went to the bottom and managed to survive.

Greta knows that whenever she feels depressed or under great stress, she can call on her self-hypnosis exercise, which, unlike drugs, is free, safe, and there is no way to overdose on it.

Marilyn also discovered the power of self-hypnosis. She was a lively 70-year-old, who had broken her ankle while race walking with a friend. Lying on a city street waiting for the ambulance, unable to move, was a traumatic experience for her. Before the accident she had been feeling terrific—years younger than her age —and had even begun taking golf lessons. Suddenly the broken ankle left her incapacitated and apprehensive.

Her ankle healed nicely and soon she was able to get about without a cane. Her problem occurred when she was forced to cross a street—and living in a pedestrian city like New York, that happened quite often. Going up a curb was fine, but going down terrified her. From her point of view, one slip would put her back in the hospital.

As we talked, I learned that Marilyn loved to dance; she had once been a dance instructor. In her self-hypnosis exercise, Marilyn began going up and down curbs as if she were performing a dance routine. In her imagination she could move and flow with the music as she went up and down the curb.

She called a week later to tell me there had been much improvement, although she still felt some fear. I explained that the concern she felt really measured how important moving freely was to her, and as she continued to move in her self-hypnosis exercise—and, increasingly, in actuality—her anxiety would slowly fade and finally leave her.

Kenneth—a television and film producer I had known for a number of years socially—suffered from a severe phobia to blood, hospitals, and needles. When he would attend a particularly gory movie, his palms would start to sweat, he wouldn't be able to catch his breath, and often he would pass out.

Kenneth had been phobic since he was a young boy. When he had to have blood drawn, he would faint. Over time he learned to accept his far-from-perfect situation. He would say to the doctors, "I'm liable to pass out when you take blood, so let me lie down." He avoided hospitals; in his worst phobic days he found it difficult to visit a friend or a loved one in a hospital. Most of the time, he couldn't get past the front door.

It was after he went to see Joe Turner's play, *Come and Gone*, on Broadway that he knew he had to seek professional help, specifically for dealing with his phobia. At the end of the play, the main character slashes his chest open with a knife and rubs blood all over his body. Kenneth fainted, and an emergency medical crew was called into the theater. His wife was really shaken up. She told him, "This has got to stop. You can't continue like this, you're going to hurt yourself."

Kenneth was aware of my work and decided to come to me. At the time, he was in therapy and often discussed his phobic problems with the therapist. The therapist was not opposed to his coming to me; in fact he encouraged Kenneth to try any avenue that might work.

Kenneth was surprised at the simplicity of self-hypnosis. "There's a lot of mumbo-jumbo written about hypnosis," he told me with wonder, "but in practice the procedure is simple, it's natural."

I explained that because he was highly hypnotizable, he would often become so absorbed with what was happening on the stage that it seemed to be happening to him. He made the fiction real and put himself into the drama. I created an exercise that helped him to distance himself from the theatrical event. The exercise was about getting perspective; it was also about control. A big issue in Kenneth's life was control over his environment. Somehow or other, he had to feel he had power over his destiny. Growing up, he felt that adults were controlling his life. His mother married a number of times and he always feared that a new man might come along and take control, and that he would have no participation in decision-making. He began to see that his blood phobia had a lot to do with this terrible fear of not having control.

In Kenneth's exercise, he imagined himself in a theater watching a play. As he sat there, he sensed himself being drawn toward the stage. At that point, an alarm would go off in his mind that told him he was being drawn out of his seat. He would take a deep breath and once again observe the play as a member of the audience.

Kenneth learned the exercise in a single session. I suggested that he could use the alarm signal device in any situation where he might be drawn in and threatened. He has used the exercise a number of times and it continues to be effective—although he called me not long ago to say that he would like a second session. Apparently he is experiencing a sort of residual effect in which his palms are still sweaty. Although he hasn't passed out since that time in the theater, on a couple of occasions he felt very claustrophobic and trapped.

He feels he needs reinforcement. In his case—because he is so highly hypnotizable—reinforcement is important so that he can more easily discriminate between illusion and reality.

Another acquaintance whom I worked with in my first year of practice was able to fight off the effects of a serious illness by using self-hypnosis—a technique she first learned in order to help her tennis game. Connie was a high-level executive widely respected in her field. She had risen from secretary to senior vice president of one of the largest clothing companies in New York and presently, she is president of her own company. She also happens to be an old friend.

As accomplished as she was in whatever area she set out to master, she suffered from a problem common to many over-achieving people: performance anxiety. On Labor Day weekend, when our families were lunching together, Connie shared her feelings of nervousness about a pending match in the finals of a charity tennis tournament. It was going to be an important culminating event of the summer season involving many of her professional friends and acquaintances; she was paired with Jason, a player who was known for his bad-boy behavior on court. She was concerned and anxious.

"What is bothering you?" I asked.

"I'm afraid he'll put me off my game and I'll play badly. A lot of people will be watching. I don't want to make a fool of myself. I don't care if we win or not, I just want to play my best game."

Connie explained that Jason's tactics could be disruptive to opponents and partners alike. She had known him for a long time, and unlike many who played with him, she wasn't particularly uncomfortable with his behavior. In fact, they had won the early rounds of the tournament despite his misbehavior. But there hadn't been a gallery of spectators during those matches. Her problem was not so much Jason as it was herself. With all those people watching, *she* would fail; *she* would blow the simplest shots. Jason, who had little patience under the best of circumstances, would heap all his scorn on her—and he would be justified. I offered Connie my professional assistance and, that same afternoon, tested her hypnotic capacity with the HIP procedure. She was very high, a solid four.

In the hypnotic exercise I gave her, Connie would visualize herself in her best form on court. She would see herself in her tennis attire, relaxed and in control —her racquet prepared, her feet perfectly positioned, her breathing even, and her concentration pure and cool. She would feel herself moving lightly on the balls of her feet. She would visualize her strokes at their very best—her forehand, backhand, her overhead and serve. The ball would look big and hitable; she would see its seams and yellow fuzz. Moving with grace, she would have all the time in the world to make a tactical decision that would put her opponents on the defensive.

I prescribed that she do the exercise herself, several times before the match. That is, she was to enter the trance state, visualize herself as the tennis player she wanted to be, enjoy and move with that image for about a minute; then exit from the trance state, while retaining the image she created.

The tournament was being held the next day, on the grounds of an elegant estate. Connie had heard all weekend about the people who were planning to attend. She kept her nervousness in check by faithfully doing the exercise I had given her: to imagine herself in charge, in control; to imagine herself concentrating, preparing, and following through with the ease of an expert.

That afternoon, she walked out onto the court in front of perhaps 100 people and she could do no wrong. She felt absolutely in touch with her game. She and Jason won the first two sets decisively. Before the third set, he told her he was going to change his strategy. He said they were winning the match too easily, that they should let up a little, have some fun and make it more interesting for the observers.

From that point on, Jason's moves became unpredictable, his behavior erratic. He made many unforced errors. Connie kept up her end as best she could under the circumstances—and even when the momentum of the match had turned against them, she was still at ease with herself and her game. Although they lost the final three sets and the match, Connie stayed within herself and her concentration never left her. Having internalized her exercise, she had become the player she envisioned. After the match, it was clear that she had won the admiration of many of the observers because she had been able to keep her cool, despite her partner's erratic performance.

The next time Connie consciously used self-hypnosis for a specific problem—again the issue was performance anxiety—she was in the process of setting up her own business. She was about to meet with potential investors, bankers, and venture capitalists—a community of professionals with whom she'd had little contact until then. The meetings were scheduled to be brief: Connie would present her ideas for starting up her own company and go over the key points of her five-year plan. Success hinged on a persuasive presentation of numbers and strategy, and she knew that she would have to perform quickly and well.

She had never been cast in the role of an entrepreneur before. Although she had always been comfortable speaking in front of people and was confident of her professional reputation, trying to raise money for a venture of her own was an entirely new—and unsettling—experience. She knew herself well enough to know that she tended to be anxious in situations where her expertise might come into question. It made her nervous that she was learning numbers and budgets for her new business from accountants and financial advisers and not from her own hands-on experience, and she wasn't sure how she'd respond to questions she was unprepared to answer.

In preparation for the meetings, she started using the self-hypnosis exercise she had learned from me, with some important differences. Instead of performing on a tennis court, she imagined herself in a conference room achieving her goals for the meeting: being seen as a knowledgeable, committed professional in her field, able to focus on planning and goals, and assured of success. She saw herself dressed in a businesslike and yet stylish and attractive fashion. She wanted to appear to the financial types who would be observing her exactly as she wanted to be seen. She did the self-hypnosis exercise several times before each meeting, sometimes in the reception area, often in the taxicab on the way there. The exercise never took more than 60 to 90 seconds. She would go into a trance and see herself in the meeting room looking and acting her optimum best; she began to feel the confidence flood through her. She knew that if the business and investment types saw this positive image of herself that she now felt so deeply, she would be able to say everything she needed to say. She would have no problem presenting the information persuasively. And it worked for her: She got and held their confidence, and she knew she'd given the meetings her best shot, regardless of the outcome. (Connie did get the backing she needed to start her own business, which continues to thrive to this day.)

Connie's third use of the self-hypnosis exercise—and by far her most crucial—came as the result of a serious illness. She was diagnosed with a rare autoimmune disease, which would be fatal unless her system responded to the only known treatment—heavy doses of steroids known to be damaging to the system. It was one of those cases where the remedy could be almost as bad as the disease. She was in a critical stage and it was not yet clear if her body would respond positively to the medication. Certain cases do not, and if the medication didn't work, there was no other known treatment.

There were, therefore, many areas of concern. The first concern was whether the medication would work at all and arrest the symptoms of the disease—fortunately it did work, as became clear in three or four days. There was also the question of whether she would continue to need high doses of the medication. Connie was in the hospital for three weeks, and had to take the medicine every day, in heavy one-time doses.

I gave Connie a self-hypnosis exercise in which she made her body receptive to the medication. She and the medication working together, would destroy and eliminate the attackers and return the immune system to its usual protective role. By being receptive to and collaborating with the medication, she could minimize the damage to her system and control the disease. That was the message each day—and many times a day. Connie would repeat: "This medicine and I are working together to heal my body. Even though this medicine can be poisonous and dangerous to me, I am taking it to help me. I am taking it so we (my body and I) will get better."

Connie's self-hypnosis exercise helped her to respond and fight a winning battle in a number of ways. For example, steroids have a tendency to bloat you, and she asked the doctors to put her on a diet. Knowing she was going to gain a lot of weight, she wanted to fight a battle on that front too, because she was in a state of wanting her body to respond. During her weeks in the hospital, she was an active participant in trying to help her body heal.

Doing her exercise three or four times a day was a way of reminding herself that she was in charge of her body. The exercise wasn't aimed just at the medication, but at the process of healing itself—with Connie as the guiding force. Connie is convinced that without the self-hypnosis exercises, the hospital experience would have been a nightmare; I am convinced of this, too. Connie believes, as I do, that with the help of self-hypnosis, the control she had over her body and mind was a key factor in her recovery.

Connie was able to find the physician within herself. It was her willingness to try to exert control over her body and mind that gave the physician within her "a chance," as Schweitzer said, "to go to work." As we will learn in the next chapter, the belief systems each one of us have are our own unique view of the world, and our behavior and attitudes are derived from that view. Rigid belief systems can lead to trouble. A supportive belief system—"I *can* take charge of my body"—helped Connie win an important battle.

Chapter 6

CHALLENGING
OUR BELIEF SYSTEMS:

*How We Can Change What We Believe
to Get What We Want*

A LOT of problems grow out of our past. They grow out
of deeply ingrained belief systems that we haven't
challenged; with guidance we can often challenge
them in a constructive way. Fear of flying, for instance,
is a particularly serious problem because it can have
grave economic consequences, which is what happened in the case of Mark.

When he first came to see me, Mark was living in
a state of fear. As he told me about a trip to Los Angeles that was coming up the following week, he literally
shook. A playwright who had had two plays produced
off-Broadway in the past year to critical acclaim, he
was suddenly considered a "hot property." His agent
had gotten him a screenplay assignment on a big-
budget Hollywood picture for which he would
earn more in three months than he had earned in the

first five years of his writing career. The hitch was, he would have to fly. And flying had become almost physically impossible for him—a form of extreme torture. His fear of flying consumed him, even in his dreams. He was fully prepared to give up the writing assignment unless I could find some way to help him.

I asked him if he believed it was dangerous to depend on someone else, and he nodded vigorously. In the case of flying, it was *damn* dangerous, he asserted. I told him that many people who are afraid to fly on commercial lines have no trouble piloting their own planes. There are others who won't travel by car unless they are driving. Didn't that suggest that the issue was not how dangerous the activity was, but rather who was in control? I suggested to Mark that one of the reasons he could not bring himself to fly was because he had difficulty sharing control over his life with other people—in this case the pilot and flight crew.

In the exercise I designed for Mark, he was to imagine himself as a passenger on a plane that had just made a smooth takeoff from Kennedy Airport. I told him that he was in charge of what he did and that if he chose to, it was within his power to turn over his need to control to the pilot. And why shouldn't the pilot be in control? He was a skilled professional who was just as concerned in reaching the designated airport as Mark was.

The exercise worked for Mark. He flew out to Los Angeles and did his 90-second exercise eight or nine times during the flight. When he called me from California, he told me, laughing, that he and the pilot had managed an extremely smooth and uneventful flight. Since Mark's breakthrough, he has become a regular commuter in the air, and he uses his self-hypnosis technique during flights to work on script ideas. During takeoff, he does his self-hypnosis exercise to help him relax and accept the transfer of control from himself to the pilot. Once he is able to accomplish that transfer, he remains in the trance-state and creates a screen on which he plays out, in a free-flowing manner, his script ideas. Dialogue and images unfold on the screen of his mind's eye. Flying time that was once given over to abject terror is now spent constructively to advance his career. With self-hypnosis, Mark has found a way to add to his own sense of self. He has managed to challenge an inflexible belief system that was doing him harm.

What are belief systems and what do they do? And what do they have to do with finding the physician within ourselves? The job ahead of us—and self-hypnosis can play a vital role here—is to be able to examine what we feel is true to see if it is, in fact, true. Is it true in every situation? Is it true for us now as adults? If my parents told me as a child that I was clumsy and couldn't do anything right, I believed them. Intellectually, I may have come to know better—as an adult I have accomplished deft and graceful physical acts— but in my gut I believe my parents. In my head, though, I want to challenge that belief, otherwise I will always be too afraid to try something I have been told I cannot do well. An important use of self-hypnosis is to assist us in taking on that challenge to change, and to make us receptive to new ideas or perspectives, which is what makes us able to change.

Many of us, like my patient George, wear a heavy set of psychological armor of which we are unaware. We carry it around with us—it impedes us. George came to me when he was 68-years-old and suffering from frequent bouts of impotence. He knew that he felt a great deal of anger toward his wife, and one of his reasons for entering therapy was to eliminate the anger. He was convinced that if he could get rid of his anger, he would stop being impotent. At the root of his problem was the conviction that he could not love someone toward whom he felt so much anger. To him, his experience demonstrated the important truth of his beliefs. He could not respond to his wife whom he loved.

George had remarried when he was 61 and his current wife was 21. He was angry because his wife and his now 19-year-old daughter from a previous marriage were constantly arguing. His wife put pressure on George to do something, and he deeply resented the pressure.

In his exercise, I asked him to imagine a large screen, such as a movie or TV screen, divided into three panels. I asked him to project the day-to-day events in his household onto the center panel. On the left-hand panel, I asked him to place those aspects of his interactions with his wife that displeased or annoyed him, and on the right-hand panel, to place those images or activities that made him feel warm, sexual, and loving toward his wife. I further explained that sometimes a single situation might appear on both the left and right panels.

George began by projecting onto the screen a fight he and his wife, Marion, had over the behavior of his daughter. At first he could only see and feel the anger, but as he looked at her, and saw how attractive she was, and how frustrated and helpless she must feel, he began warming to her. Next, he saw himself coming home to a special dinner Marion had prepared and he felt a rush of warmth. He saw them going for walks and visiting friends. As their life was projected onto the screen, George saw Marion in all her dimensions and he could feel love and warmth flowing through him.

With the help of the exercise, George learned to separate the things that made him angry from the things that attracted him to his wife and made him feel loving toward her. Regaining his potency was an expression of his new recognition that, on occasion, it was natural—it was okay—to feel anger toward someone you loved. Anger and love *could* coexist. By challenging his belief, he was able to change it.

Eileen was an attractive 28-year-old musician. She had always thought of herself as a person for whom creativity flowed bountifully—that it was always at her beck and call. For the past year, she had been working on a long commissioned theater piece that seemed to be "composing itself." And then, suddenly, the flow was gone; her inspiration had dried up. It was as though a blind had been drawn, leaving her mind in darkness. She could no longer write a note of music and was in a state of panic. She suffered from a belief system that said to her, "Eileen, you must always be a model to others; A model of competency and control." She perceived the dying out of her creative spark as a failure of character. In desperation, she looked around for help. After reading an article on hypnosis, she came to see me.

She was the oldest of four children: two boys and two girls. Her father was a business consultant and traveled a great deal; her mother was a fabric designer. Both parents were well educated. From the beginning, Eileen was "the brilliant one," the child of whom much was expected, and emotionally demanded. She was a straight A student throughout high school and college, and her parents' expectations for her career were of the highest order. I suspected that it was from concern of not pleasing them that she never stopped working, never took a vacation. However, when she found herself blocked in her work, she immediately blamed herself: She was secretly "lazy." Patients often blame themselves for any failure to perform; they accuse themselves of being lazy or lacking will power. They need some explanation that makes sense to them, and leaves them in control. If what is happening is their fault, then at least *they* are still in control. All they have to do is act correctly and problems will dissolve.

Eileen usually worked in her studio from one to six in the afternoon, five days a week, and would spend the rest of her time cleaning house, or reading, or going to museums or lectures: constantly improving herself. In the midst of her creative drought, she kept up with her other activities—and even accelerated them because she could not face her studio and her failure to produce. Whenever she made an effort to compose, she felt as though she was fighting off extreme exhaustion, flu symptoms, or a vague but deep-seated panic.

When I questioned her, Eileen was unable to think of anything in her life that was disturbing her except for her creative block. She loved her parents, she got along well with her siblings, and she had a satisfying, long-standing relationship with a fellow musician. She insisted that except for her inability to create, she would not change her life in any way.

I taught her to use self-hypnosis to place herself in trance and walk herself down an imaginary flight of stairs to a very safe and comfortable place—a place where she felt totally at ease within herself. Once in her safe place, I asked her to sit in a comfortable chair facing a screen, which was divided into three panels. She was to take her daily experiences and project them onto the middle panel. Then, as she studied that panel, she was to transfer to the left-hand panel those things that disturbed or upset her, things that made her angry or sad. On the right-hand panel, she was to place those things that pleased her and made her feel creative and good about herself.

As Eileen viewed her daily activities and her contact with her parents on the screen, she could feel how much her life had been involved in trying to please them. She was drawn to images of her childhood—scenes where she lorded it over her brother and sister (in one scene she visualized on the screen, she had them bring her ice cream on a tray and call her "Your Highness"). She saw how she used music to win the love and attention of her parents. She was bothered that whenever she had to make a decision, she thought in terms of what would please her parents, rather than what would please herself. As she studied the right-hand panel with scenes of her working on a composition and hearing the music performed, she realized how pleased she was with her ability to create, and how important it was to her.

When Eileen called to set up a second appointment, there was excitement and new life in her voice. I could feel her vibrancy over the phone. She told me that the three-panel exercise had been a revelation. "There's so much I've been hiding from myself," she told me. "For years I've been writing music for my parents, not for me. I saw this clearly in the exercise. It just popped up there. Also, instead of just loving my brothers and sisters for the people they are and taking a real interest in their lives, I've been in this tremendous competition with them. I've had to prove to them how great I am, how brilliant. I've been on trial. It was all there—on the screen." She began to sob. "But on the right-hand panel, there was so little. There just weren't that many things that made me feel good about myself. . . ."

"Facing the truth is a beginning," I told her.

"But I did see my work on that screen," she said, suddenly animated again. "I feel eager for the first time in a long time. I think I'm about to get back to my music."

Through hypnosis, Eileen had found the physician within herself.

I am often asked why, even when we feel that our behavior makes no sense, we continue to act in ways that are destructive to our goals. Do we self-destruct as a way to punish ourselves? I think that to answer that question we have to take a look at the way in which we develop. At every stage of growth, starting in infancy, we develop a personal model of the world —a gut interpretation. From the beginning, we seem to need to explain why things happen: Why someone comes to feed us or pick us up when we cry; why mommy sometimes feels anxious and at other times warm and loving; why people yell or get excited; why we are soothed. It would appear that we need to know in order to feel safe.

Children initially believe—and for the infant it is a reasonable conclusion—that the world revolves around them. They cry and someone is there to soothe them. Their needs and wants are satisfied immediately. Of course, before too long, the child becomes aware that sometimes when he cries, this nurturing person—mother, father, nursemaid—does not respond immediately. The child then has to begin to deal with the complexity of the behavior of others and accept the anxiety that accompanies the knowledge that they are not in control. The child's curiosity—its wondering—is in part stimulation, in part exploration, and in part a need to build a model of the world. He progresses from the stage of playing at his mother's feet to moving a distance from the mother, turning around to see if she is still present, and eventually moving out of her orbit, occasionally returning to check on her, then feeling more comfortable about playing in another environment. The ever-widening circles of independence continue throughout childhood.

As the child has explored and tested the world and begun to develop a point of view about how the world works, he has learned a valuable rule of existence: it is okay to go this distance from the mother and she will still be present. Although the child is not aware of the rule, it has nonetheless become an integral part of his perception of the world and of his behavior. The child who explores and finds that when he returns, the mother is not there, develops a different set of rules, a different belief system. He begins to wonder whether the mother will or will not be there when he returns. Each time he leaves, there is a level of anxiety about the mother's presence or absence.

Psychologists L. Joseph Stone and Joseph Church in their work *Childhood and Adolescence: A Psychology of the Growing Person*, wrote:

> Underlying the specific development [of language and motor skills] is a more general kind of learning that pervades all the baby's emerging relationships with his environment. This is the learning

not of specific skills or acts, but of basic attitudes of trust or distrust toward the whole world, which [Erik H.] Erikson postulates as the first of a series of critical alternatives arising during development. The infant first becomes aware of the environment in terms of the way it meets his physical and emotional needs. If his needs are attended to fully and dependably, he becomes aware of the world as a good, stable, safe, encouraging place to be—a place to be trusted. When his needs are not met, the world comes within his ken as a frustrating, threatening place where no trust is possible. This essential learning exists in a pervasive parent's touch, and not just physiological relief, that conveys stability, security, warmth and, affection, that tells the baby the world can be trusted.

When some of these children (the ones who perceive of themselves as abandoned) end up as my patients, they request that I get rid of their anxiety. They also hope I can use hypnosis to instantly eliminate such feelings as love, anger, and hate—the dangerous and threatening emotions. I explain to them that the only way to eliminate feelings is to eliminate the person. Feelings are like an instrument in that they measure, with precision, the inner atmosphere; they tell us how we feel about our environment and relationships. The problem is that most of us do not know how to connect effectively with our feelings. In order to use them for our benefit, we have to understand where they come from; only then, and over time, can we change our reactions to a given situation. Only then can behavior stemming from inappropriate belief systems be successfully modified.

Besides individual and family belief systems, there are pervasive societal beliefs. It is common to hear parents tell their children, "You're not supposed to be angry. You shouldn't feel angry. You're not supposed to be running around playing and shouting. you're not supposed to want something all the time."

Another widely-held belief is that men are not supposed to cry. To cry is to be stripped of your manhood. Even today with attitudes toward gender more sophisticated than ever before, women operate under a different set of rules. It is okay for women to feel, to be emotional, to cry. In order to challenge that belief system, we have to ask ourselves, why the difference? Aren't we all human beings? Don't men have emotions? Feeling the pressure of that particular societal belief system, men will often answer "no." If a man shows too much emotion, especially tenderness or sensitivity, there is something wrong with him. It is a weakness that he has to hide. If you believe having feelings is wrong and a weakness, you hide your feelings. You don't expose them; you bury them beneath banter or wit or stoicism, which are all manly virtues. Sometimes you even hide them from yourself.

It starts when we are young. A key commandment of the belief system is that boys don't cry. How many times have we heard that boys—real boys—don't cry? The parent says, not necessarily in words but in clear unspoken messages, "It upsets me when you cry. What are the other kids going to think? You're not going to get any sympathy from *them*. Learn to control yourself!" Of course the boy absorbs the belief system into himself. He feels heroic when he can stop himself; he has become a full-fledged man of the tribe. God has announced the way of the world: Real boys don't cry; real men don't eat quiche.

The ways we lead our lives are guided by belief systems. Many are helpful; others get in the way or are harmful and must be challenged for our own well-being; and still others are relatively insignificant. For example, if you believe that sleeping on the right side of the bed rather than the left makes a difference, so what? It doesn't hurt you. What we call superstitions are actually minor belief systems that society has agreed make little sense. On the other hand, we do not call the belief system that men shouldn't cry a superstition because society agrees that they shouldn't cry. Although it's not more true than any of the other superstitions, it is widely believed and therefore elevated to the status of a truth.

Many beliefs are basically useful, but need adjustments in order to correspond more closely to reality. For example, when my children were young, I made them participate in housework. My belief system dictated that they should do chores without grumbling. They should accept the fact that housework was a real responsibility and be proud of their share in doing it. As I grew to understand my own beliefs better and challenged many of them, I still very much believed they should participate in the housework—but with a difference. Now, when they grumbled it was easy for me to say to them, "you don't have to like it, you just have to do it." There was no longer a requirement that they accept housework as something wonderful; it is not a wonderful task. It was enough that they accepted responsibility for doing the work; they didn't have to like it. In fact, their not liking it was *perfectly legitimate*. For most people, there is not much gratification involved in housework, nor is there anything particularly moral or uplifting in vacuuming carpets or washing dishes. We didn't like it when we were children—why should our children be any different? It is simply there to be done, with or without grumbling. But many of us hold to the belief system that doing the job isn't enough; we have to love it too. If, however, you let the person do the job on his or her own terms, you legitimize that person. An appropriate belief system legitimizes both you and the person affected by your beliefs. My belief that you have a right to your own feelings about something is a nurturing belief.

When Anthony came to me, he was in a state of great distress following a series of misunderstandings with his new girlfriend Hilda, a successful Manhattan accountant. His trouble had come to a head one night when they had made plans to have dinner out; they agreed to meet on a certain New York City street corner. Half an hour passed and he became extremely annoyed. He admitted that when people are late he reacts very badly. Standing there waiting, he had the need to find an explanation for why she was late. Seeking to justify his feelings—simply being annoyed because she was late didn't seem adequate, especially to Anthony in his considerably annoyed state—he took the position that she was acting maliciously. Bluntly put, she didn't care enough about him to be on time. That belief—which indeed held promise as an option —could have stemmed from experiences in Anthony's childhood when, he told me, he felt anxious and no one acted to help. He assumed that those he loved and was dependent on didn't care sufficiently about his welfare.

Anthony was operating from a core belief, which was: If you truly care about me, you will never do anything that makes me feel anxious. If Anthony chose to maintain that belief, he was going to be very, very angry with Hilda for mistreating him and would end up swept along on a great wave of self-pity. But he had another option. If instead of accepting and justifying the little-boy-lost posture, he chose to ask her, "Why are you late?" he would be on his way to challenging that belief. Rather than ranting and justifying greater ranting, he would learn what happened so that he could base his judgment on his partner's response. If he did that often enough, he would begin to realize that any unchallenged belief system can be a poor predictor of what actually happens.

And what proved to be the actual facts that unsettling evening as Anthony waited on the corner battling his anger? As he explained toward the end of our first session, Hilda was caught up in work at the office and totally lost track of the time. She was wrestling with a complex accounting problem—and it was one she was less likely to share with him once he showed his anger. She was obviously upset at having kept him waiting, and it was clear she was not acting in a way that was designed to injure him. They both knew he tended to get annoyed at being kept waiting, especially in uncomfortable situations. I explained to Anthony that his annoyance was something she would have to learn to acknowledge whenever she arrived late. By the same token, he would have to learn to tolerate her lateness and understand that whenever she was deeply involved, she lost track of time.

Once you understand your own belief system, you can move ahead and discover what is actually happening. You can respond to the behavior that annoys you with questions rather than assume answers. You can create a self-hypnosis exercise to explore scenarios in which the other person fulfills her goals and you yours, and where you won't constantly feel hurt. In the case of Anthony and Hilda, they agreed to stop meeting on street corners. They picked comfortable restaurants where it's possible to sit and relax. Anthony found a way to change the scenario so that it no longer easily supported or promoted negative feelings. The way to change a belief is to modify the behavior that supports the belief. By asking Hilda why she was late—instead of acting as if he knew—he was challenging his belief that lateness is always a malicious act.

We expect somehow that we should be able to simply say to ourselves "stop being anxious," "don't be angry," or "it's no big thing." However, while you're waiting on a street corner for the person you love who is not on time, it is very difficult to convince yourself. Our feelings are not dictated by "shoulds" or "should nots." A recent study by psychologist Joseph LeDoux, at New York University's Centre for Neural Science, suggests that emotional reactions occur before the brain has even had time to fully register what it is that is causing the reaction. He believes that early memories and experiences, a key to emotional life, are stored as visceral rather than cognitive memories, and for that reason are especially difficult to change.

What Anthony felt waiting on the street corner was complex. He was anxious and uncomfortable. Because he hated to be anxious and uncomfortable, he was also angry—that was his gut reaction. His gut was telling him how it felt about the situation. His mind was also at work, drawing on his history and beliefs. A complex scenario was being played out in his head, but *he had left out the other person.*

When we acknowledge our feelings but also stop and ask the other person what happened and what they feel, we are challenging our own history and beliefs. We are admitting that the scenario played out in our head may be wrong. What we've learned to do is question, and that questioning can become our doorway to freedom.

Anthony changed the way he felt and acted by adding new ideas and perspectives. Our responses are based on our view of a situation. our expectations, and our understanding. Modify the way you see a situation and your response will change. Milton Erickson states that

> Therapy results from an inner resynthesis of the patient's behavior achieved by the patient himself. It's true that *direct* suggestion can effect an alteration in the patient's behavior and result in a symptomatic cure, at least temporarily. However, such a "cure," is simply a response to suggestion and does not entail that reassociation and reorganization of ideas, understandings and memories so essential for actual cure.

Our belief systems also affect the way we respond to stress. Bill, a lawyer working with a prestigious Wall Street firm, came to me in a state of extreme apprehension. His position with the firm depended on his passing the bar and getting his license, and he had tried twice before and failed. His nervousness and anxiety had been building for weeks before the examination.

I explained to Bill that anxiety can be a useful and important survival tool. Used appropriately, it could help him pass the exam. Research has shown that individuals who are slightly anxious before an examination do better than those without any anxiety at all as well as those who are *too* tense. Anxiety is a healthy, normal reaction to any potentially dangerous situation. It is also a healthy, normal reaction to situations that we see as important. In fact, the level of anxiety we experience is probably proportional to the level of importance. Passing the bar exam was obviously very important to Bill. The problem with anxiety, however, comes when we believe—as Bill obviously did—that our anxiety is a warning or premonition of disaster. Then healthy anxiety is transformed into a debilitating panic response.

As the time to take the bar examination grew closer, Bill was saying to himself, "I'm afraid of this exam. I know I can't pass it. Look what happened before." Thus he established a self-fulfilling prophecy. He began to transform his natural state of anxiety into crippling fear, and was certain he wouldn't be able to deal with the material. In fact, however, his anxiety was simply an expression of how important passing the bar examination was too him. But instead of perceiving the problem in its true light, Bill viewed it as dangerous and threatening. He then moved from a state of alertness—which would make all the information available to him—to one of hyperanxiety. As he entered the examination room, he began to panic. Once he was in the grip of panic, all of the knowledge pathways became blocked. The fact that he felt deep in his gut he would fail the exam became exactly the mechanism by which he was unable to pass it. No lack of knowledge or information defeated him, but rather his sense that the situation was *out of his control.*

Hypnosis helped Bill to gain a sense of his own power and control. The anxiety remained—the anxiety that kept his sharpness at its peak. In the self-hypnosis exercise I gave Bill, he imagined himself focused and thoughtful, working hard to pass the exam. He also imagined himself walking into a comfortable and yet stylish, brightly-lit office—*his* private office. He had passed the bar exam with flying colors and knew that his law firm would place him on the partnership track. He was already on the rise, with employers who valued his intelligence and poise, and clients who looked to him for sound advice. The exercise helped Bill to restructure in his own mind the bar examination problem and to view it in terms of positive results (he would become a practicing lawyer), rather than in terms of its danger (he would fail and become nothing). As stated earlier, there is little doubt that the way in which we perceive an event—not in our minds, but in our gut—has a decided influence on the way we behave and therefore on the outcome.

We sometimes don't realize that the anxiety we're experiencing, the state of heightened awareness, is a very useful and important tool. It's a normal reaction when the situation is important to us, or new and unfamiliar. Most of us were anxious on our first date, the first time we took a downhill slope on skis, the first day we went to school, the first day on the job. It is easy to confuse anxiety with fear. The emotions we feel are a reflection of bodily experiences—changes in blood pressure, heart rate, and breathing—and whether you're running in a marathon or fleeing from a mugger, your body's responses appear to be the same. Yet in the first instance you are anxious to win, to do your best, while in the case of the mugger you're frightened of being hurt. Your body reacts in the same way to two very different situations. Anxiety is the appropriate response to the marathon; fear is the appropriate response to the mugger. However, we often confuse the two responses in a way that does us harm.

By turning anxiety into a fear response, Bill was suffering from "stage fright." We've all heard the term which is essentially the anxiety of a performer wanting to give a superior performance. The problem comes when we begin to interpret that emotional response and explain it to ourselves. That's what happened to Bill. And in the British movie, *The Dresser*, it happens to a Shakespearean actor in a small English traveling company who begins to worry about his lines days before he performs in a role he has played many times. He doesn't realize he's experiencing a natural state of anxiety that stems from a desire to do his best. The trouble begins when he explains that feeling in terms of fear. Slowly the conviction grows in him that he will forget his lines; his belief system creates a blueprint for failure. Never mind that as a seasoned professional who has repeated that performance perhaps 1000 times he is likely to sail through the performance with no problems. Driven by his own belief system, he transforms the anxiety into fear. The fear builds to the point where he *knows* he will forget his lines. Fear can turn the direst possibilities into probabilities. Drowned in his worries, he begins to drink. The actor has taken the power the body has given him for normal heightened alertness, and instead of using that power to help develop the most effective performance, he uses it in a destructive way. He believes that being anxious is a predictor of doom. He believes that if you're anxious, something bad is bound to happen to you. Thus by treating his anxiety as a justifiable fear, the actor creates a self-fulfilling prophecy. He panics; he blows his lines.

In real life, Derek Jacobi, one of England's premier actors, suffered from similar fears, as he explained in a 1988 newspaper interview. One evening, while waiting in the wings to begin a performance of Hamlet, he wondered what would happen if he forgot his lines. His imagination took flight, producing an anxiety which intensified to become a "gut-wrenching terror." It took him four years to overcome the belief that we all probably need to challenge: When I get anxious, I know something bad will happen.

We make the mistake of attaching a negative value to anxiety. We feel uncomfortable when we are anxious. We don't see any difference between anxiety and fear because, as stated earlier, we can't *feel* a difference. All of us remember being anxious on our first date. Why? Were we going to be locked in a torture chamber? No. We were anxious because the date was important to us. We hoped to make a good impression, to be charming, to be liked. In such situations our body becomes hyperalert so we can function most effectively.

Why do you look both ways when you come to a corner? Because you feel enough anxiety to sense the warning signal: be careful, a car could strike you down. There is also an element of fear involved in walking the streets of any big city, but I would call that reasonable fear. Cities can be dangerous, especially at night, and it's prudent to feel a moderate charge of fear. When I drive a car I experience anxiety, but I don't validate that feeling as a predictor of an accident; it's simply a concern for my safety, a recognition of possible danger. Emotions, such as anxiety, are what nature has given us to rapidly and intuitively survey a situation. Our emotional reactions put us on alert, but we gain little from jumping to wrong conclusions. We need to remember that just because we *feel* something unsettling, we don't automatically need to become afraid. By applying judgment and experience, we can successfully challenge damaging beliefs such as, "If I'm anxious there must be something wrong."

Alicia managed to challenge a stubborn belief system of another kind. A 50-year-old grammar-school teacher, she came to me because she was having increasing difficulty controlling her incontinence when in front of the class. Exhaustive tests revealed no medical basis for her problem.

It was clear during the first session that she disliked herself. It is sad to see patients (and I often do) who dislike themselves so much they wish they were someone else. These patients judge qualities within themselves, such as caring about others or having a strong sense of responsibility, as negative rather than positive. They become angry at themselves and feel that their altruism and extreme conscientiousness leave them open to criticism. They wish they could be like other people, who appear to them less vulnerable.

Alicia had a son who hated school, a marriage that was in trouble, and parents who were critical of everything she did. To make matters worse, her parents lived downstairs. It seemed that the whole world was dumping on her and nothing was easier than for Alicia to join the abuse by urinating on herself.

I gave her an exercise in which she was to imagine that she was her own best friend who was having a specific difficulty. She loved and respected her friend; now what could she do to help her? How would she go about treating this needy human being in a loving, respectful, and protective manner? I asked Alicia if she would be abusive toward her "friend," or overly critical. She indicated that with others she was usually understanding and constructive. I think helping Alicia to see herself as someone she could care about turned her problem around. As she began to care for herself and truly take loving responsibility for her body, her incontinence ended.

Belief systems impact on all aspects of our lives, big and small. For example, traffic jams are a helpful illustration of how they can work either for or against us. There are two things that can promote anger as you sit in your car waiting to move: One, you're caught in a traffic jam, smelling exhaust fumes and listening to the blaring of horns, and two, you feel there's nothing you can do about it.

Contrary to the wide-spread belief that people will not be angered by unpleasant events unless they are attributed to someone's intentional and controllable misdeed, Leonard Berkowitz has recently published an impressive study that shows "both physical discomfort and thoughts of unpleasant occurrences" can activate angry feelings and ideas.

A traffic jam is definitely an "unpleasant occurrence." Anger and a feeling of impotence feed on each other. Anger ranges from simple annoyance to rage. First you're annoyed, but you push the feeling away . . . then you feel helpless and this feeling of helplessness makes you even angrier. Before you know it, you're in a rage. Stalled traffic becomes simply another example of how things always seem to go wrong for you. In a traffic jam, everyone is impotent. At first, the person who always feels a sense of impotence may try to deny his anger. His belief system tells him that *feeling angry in a traffic jam is wrong.* Perhaps his father told him it was manly to hold in his anger while driving a car. Or perhaps his mother drummed into him that it was bad manners to lose control of his emotions, or that if you can't do anything about a situation, you shouldn't be angry. But what is wrong with being annoyed in a traffic jam? What could be more natural than feeling annoyed when cars slow down and you're doing two miles an hour, and the noise, the heat, and the exhaust fumes are stifling? What's wrong with accepting your feelings of annoyance and acknowledging that an unpleasant situation is upsetting to you? When you continually deny feelings of anger, you are burying a natural emotional reaction, and building up an inner rage until finally it bursts out of you. You start screaming, pounding the steering wheel, and uttering a stream of obscenities—none of which have anything to do with the traffic jam. Your rage has to do with your feelings of impotence.

It's the old story—the belief that nice people shouldn't get angry. Let's say that you come into my office, sit in my chair, and start to scratch the leather with your fingernail. It bothers me, but because I'm not *allowed* to be angry I can't simply say, "Please stop doing that. It annoys me," even though it's an appropriate response and should be sufficient to solve the problem. If I can't allow myself to say something to you, the next time you come, you are likely to continue scratching the leather. Now I'm angry at you and I'm also angry at myself because I said nothing to you on your first visit. *I was a great guy for not getting angry before and yet you're still mutilating my chair.* I've made myself impotent; I'm feeling four times angrier right now than I believe I should feel, and four times more annoyed than I felt the first time. To complicate matters further, I can no longer say anything because I'm afraid you'll see how angry I am and you'll think I'm crazy. By the third time you come in, I feel totally impotent; now I want to murder you. This is the kind of illogical thinking we operate under when we adopt belief systems that inhibit normal responses. Because I labored under a belief system that limited a normal range of expression, I ended up in a rage about trivial behavior; I acted in a way that was worthy neither of you, nor me. If I had said something to you initially, you probably would have stopped scratching the leather; I would have reacted reasonably, and you wouldn't have resented my telling you.

A patient of mine, Richard, often became angry and anxious if his girlfriend, Betty, was not at home when he called. He would automatically promote beliefs that justified his anger. She knew I was going to call tonight, he would reason, and just didn't care if she spoke to me. Betty doesn't really love me. She's out with another guy. I can't trust her. When Richard would finally get her on the telephone, he would say nothing of what he was feeling, because he also believed that if you express your anger, people will leave you. However, as it usually does, his anger came through, taking the form of withdrawal and distance. See how nice he was? He didn't act angry. His way to deal with his anger was to hide it, to be silent, a silent sufferer. Internally, however, he was in a rage. Throughout his life, his girlfriends had often told him that he was an inaccessible person. However, this time he wanted to avoid the self-fulfilling prophecy that Betty didn't love him.

This is not to say that rage is always misplaced, or is only an expression of impotence. When you see someone attack a small child, an old person, or a loved one, rage is instantaneous; it is anger at a level appropriate to the situation.

We all need outlets for our feelings and flexible belief systems allow us these outlets. No matter how close two people are, they will do things that bother each other. If Amy can say, "John, that bothers me, please don't do it," chances are John will stop doing it unless it's very important to him, in which case he'll say, "Look, I'm sorry that bothers you, Amy, but I think it's important." They have been honest with each other and are now in a position to negotiate through discussion and compromise. If, however, Amy's belief system doesn't allow her the right to be annoyed, then she can't say anything to John. In all likelihood, if she doesn't tell him what bothers her, he'll keep on doing it and her anger will build to an inappropriate level.

Just as unreasonable belief systems can prevent us from feeling what I call appropriate anger, so can they demand that we overcome every fear. The inflexible belief system states: A real man does not fear anything. If he does, he's not a real man. I like to use the example of the airplane and the roller coaster to illustrate how unreasonable belief systems can lead to unnecessary complications. Many people are afraid of flying and probably just as many are afraid of roller coasters. They both seem to be risky ventures, though statistically there are very few fatalities either in the air or out at the fairground. The difference between riding a plane or a roller coaster, however, is one of value. Most of us need to fly for professional, social, and recreational reasons. Because it's the fastest means of travel and represents an extreme economy of time, it's imperative to overcome a fear of flying. But a roller coaster ride has no particular value; there is no need to fight against the fear of going up and down in a small car on narrow tracks to the sound of screaming kids. But here again, the unreasonable belief system comes into play. The man says, "I have to show everyone that I'm a man, and a real man cannot possibly fear a roller coaster." And so as much as the roller coaster fills him with terror, he has to take the ride, even at the risk of a heart attack.

Belief systems can be carried on to the next generation. Just as the father has to pretend to like the "risk-taking" behavior of the roller coaster (as stated earlier; real boy's don't cry, real men don't eat quiche), so it is likely that his son will follow suit. In the movie *Harry and the Hendersons*, the father teaches his son to shoot game. He has a macho attitude about hunting that his pre-teen son mimics in an unconsciously exaggerated way. When Henderson tells his son that they're going for a kill, the boy reacts with a kind of bloodthirsty glee. He is eager to appear as macho as his father. There are, of course, men who love hunting, and some make their living from the sport. For them, pursuit of game is not tied to an inflexible belief system, but in Henderson's case it is. As a boy he wanted to be a painter, but his father was utterly opposed to it. He considered painting a "feminine" activity and attempted to instill in Henderson the "manly virtues." He took the unwilling boy hunting, and by the time the boy became a man, he was teaching *his* son to be a hunter. Harry, the furry monster of the title, enters the Henderson family and worms his way into their affections. He buries all the mounted trophy-room "kills" in the back yard. He shocks Henderson into confronting the truth about his double life. Henderson realizes that more than anything he wants to paint Harry. Killing the monster is the furthest thing from his mind. He also realizes that he is doing to his son exactly what his father did to him: forcing him to grow into the kind of man who has to test himself constantly, whether or not the testing has any intrinsic worth or meaning. He has been the victim of a common fallacy: Real men love to hunt.

There are a number of common fallacies that all of us use to support our beliefs.

For example:

1. If I feel bad, I must have done something wrong.
2. I can't act any differently—it's the way I feel.
3. Whenever something bad happens, I know I'm being punished.
4. If something goes wrong, someone must be at fault. Either it's me or someone else.
5. If it's not perfect, it's not right.
6. Anyone who gets anxious is really sick.
7. When I'm anxious, I know that something bad will happen.
8. I need to be 100 percent sure I'm right before I do anything.
9. People should be fair.
10. People who love me should always understand me.
11. I can control the way I feel and how others feel. All I have to do is keep trying.
12. Problems can be solved by will power alone.
13. If something feels true, it *is* true.
14. You can't really trust anyone.
15. I said that to you because I was only trying to help.
16. You always know what someone feels. You never need to ask.
17. You know that if you're good and kind, only good things will happen to you.
18. Things always seem to go wrong for me.
19. People never appreciate what you do for them.
20. I can't allow myself to love too much because I'll end up hurt.

These widely-held fallacies provide social support and help to perpetuate our personal belief systems.

Miriam could never ask favors of people, even those closest to her, for fear that they would be angry with her and therefore refuse to help. During our first therapy session, I suggested Miriam put that proposition to a valid test. At first she might expose her vulnerability with people whose reactions would be likely to hurt her the least. I remember how surprised she was when, at the next session, she told me it had worked. She had not believed it possible that people would actually be happy to help her.

She was the victim of the fallacy, "I can't act any differently, it's the way I feel." That's why, even when she met people who were willing to do favors, she could never bring herself to ask. Even when Miriam started asking and often found that people were happy to help her, it took her a while to feel it was OK to ask.

To support her reaching out to others and to challenge her personal version of the common fallacy, Miriam and I created a self-hypnosis exercise in which she would see herself reaching out to a new person and recalling, visually and viscerally, the wonderful way she felt about herself and the other person.

In the exercise, she also incorporated the discomfort she felt when she started to ask for a favor and the way she felt when she first realized that the person she had asked had refused—not because he was angry, but because he just didn't want to help.

Miriam also realized she would always feel somewhat awkward asking for favors; that was part of her personal history. But now, for the first time, she understood she could act in a way that supported her goals despite her personal feelings.

As you can see from the list of fallacies, many of

our more rigid and unproductive beliefs involve a fear of not being in control as well as a failure to take risks. A patient of mine finally understood the importance of risk-taking enough to give me the following poem, which was signed Anonymous:

> *To laugh—*
>   *is to risk appearing the fool.*
> *To weep—*
>   *is to risk appearing sentimental.*
> *To reach out for another—*
>   *is to risk involvement.*
> *To expose feelings—*
>   *is to risk exposing our true self.*
> *To place your ideas, your dreams before the crowd—*
>   *is to risk loss.*
> *To love—*
>   *is to risk not being loved in return.*
> *To live—*
>   *is to risk dying.*
> *To hope—*
>   *is to risk despair.*
> *To try—*
>   *is to risk failure.*
> *But risk we must—*
>   *because the greatest hazard in life is to*
>   *risk nothing. The man, the woman who risks*
>   *nothing has nothing, is nothing.*

It's important to keep in mind that many of our beliefs are both legitimate and sensible—it is safer to stop for a red light than to run it; it is dangerous to drive while drunk; it is wrong to starve or beat your children; it is healthy to get proper rest; and it is dangerous to your health to smoke cigarettes. Belief systems, good and bad, are rules we live by, and what we believe affects how we perceive a situation and behave in it.

Through self-hypnosis, you can learn what your belief systems are and, when necessary, modify them. But as I stated earlier, self-hypnosis is only one of many techniques that can help you change your behavior and deal more effectively with your problems. We will now examine some of the alternative techniques available to you.

Chapter 7

OTHER DOORWAYS
INTO THE SAME ROOM

ALTHOUGH I work with hypnosis, I was also trained as a psychoanalyst, and analysis is one aspect of my practice. I believe there are patients for whom it is the most appropriate—and perhaps the only effective—method. I feel that analysis is indicated for patients with severe character or mood disorders, as well as for those suffering from obsessional and phobic states. Problems that impair personal growth and the development of relationships—and which tend to be both diffuse and chronic—may well require the transferential, insight-oriented, discovery approach provided by analysis. Furthermore, it is often the first choice of any individual who sees the comprehensive understanding of self as the best vehicle for change.

Everyone trained in psychotherapy acknowledges a debt to Sigmund Freud; his was the subtlest of minds and he was preeminent in the world of psychology. It was his mandate to improve his patients' mental condition, and, to accomplish this, he had the courage to reach into uncharted areas of the unconscious mind.

Although many therapists quarrel with Freud's theories of what lies at the core of our problems and many even have reservations about the need to *reach* the core, Freud led the way in showing us that hidden thoughts and feelings could influence bodily responses and behavior.

Much has been written on psychoanalytic therapy; I would like to add only the following perspective. Although Freud was known to reject the use of hypnosis early in his career, current psychoanalytic practice need not be so limited. A number of colleagues trained in the analytic approach have used hypnosis as an adjunct to therapy, as I do in my own analytic practice. I have also been called upon to provide that service for other analysts. When the patient or therapy is immobilized by acute psycho-physical problems that may be susceptible to hypnotic or other forms of short-term treatment, analysts should not be bound rigidly by history or ancestry. Change is the inevitable law of nature. The only question is direction. Even Freud in his 1919 paper "Turnings in the Ways of Analysis" acknowledged a need for other therapeutic approaches. He spoke of blending "the pure gold of analysis plentifully with the copper of direct suggestion." He foresaw the eventual incorporation of hypnosis, and other problem-oriented, short term approaches into the process of psychotherapy. These techniques are doorways into the same inner room where we are able to communicate with all aspects of the self—body and mind.

SHORT-TERM THERAPY

The goal of short-term therapy is to restructure or reframe a problem situation so that the effective resolution of the problem can be seen by the patient. I have a number of patients who see me on a short-term basis, as needed. They come in, we have a few sessions, and then they return a year later for one or two sessions because once again they have an issue they chose to deal with.

A patient may come to me because she's thinking of changing jobs. Should she or shouldn't she? Indecision is causing her excessive anxiety and she needs someone as a sounding board to raise questions and help clarify for her what the issues are. If we successfully resolve the job question, that may be the end of therapy for the present. She's going to go out and apply what she's learned to life. A year or two later, she may telephone me and ask for other sessions because a new issue has come into play. We may work together for two, 10, or 20 sessions and again, the sessions will be focused on a specific issue she chooses to deal with. If other issues arise, she may say, "I really don't want to go into that right now. I know I've got problems with my family, but I can live with it. When I'm ready I'll come back and see you." Unless the patient is in danger, the therapist's primary responsibility is to be sure the patient is informed. The patient then can make the choice.

Short-term therapies, of which self-hypnosis is one technique, have been criticized for focusing on the patient's symptoms rather than on the patient as a whole. It is argued that if you get rid of one symptom, the patient will only develop another one; you cannot really solve the patient's problem by eliminating symptoms. There is, however, substantial clinical evidence to contradict that point of view. Behavior modification techniques (including self-hypnosis) have alleviated symptoms for a multitude of patients and allowed them to take on more productive lives. Many are afflicted by phobias—phobias of heights, depths, colors, cats and cars—and, after years of treatment to unearth the root of the phobia, some may still be left with the problem even though they may have learned a great deal about themselves in the process. The phobias present real and immediate dangers to them, and the results can be economically, as well as emotionally, devastating. If you suffer from agoraphobia (fear of being in an open space) and can't leave your house to go to work, you're not likely to have a wide range of career choices. Yes, it is true that change can bring new problems and perhaps other symptoms. However, the goal of therapy is to teach patients techniques they can use to deal with problems, to eliminate them when possible or at least alleviate them, or perhaps just to change their destructive effect.

In most schools of short-term therapy, the fundamental issues dealt with in treatment are self-realization, self-improvement, and management of stress. In these therapies, there is an interactive relationship between therapist and patient; the treatment is at root existential in that the actual is favored over the conceptual. The patient can "learn" what the therapist "teaches."

There are numerous forms of short-term "talking" therapies that can help to alleviate specific problems. The eclectic therapist may combine and incorporate techniques drawn from cognitive therapy (Albert Ellis and Aaron T. Beck), from short-term dynamic psychotherapy (Habib Davenloo and Peter E. Sifneos), and therapeutic hypnosis (Milton Erickson, Ernest L. Rossi, and Herbert Spiegel).

MEDITATION TECHNIQUES

While searching for behavioral techniques for lowering blood pressure, the physician Herbert Benson (author of *The Relaxation Response*) studied Transcendental Meditation. Benson was impressed by the simplicity of the technique. "A trained instructor gives you a secret word or sound or phrase, a mantra, which you promise not to divulge . . . The meditator receives the mantra from his teacher and repeats it mentally over and over again while sitting in a comfortable position. The purpose of the repetition is to prevent distracting thoughts. Meditators are told to assume a passive attitude and if other thoughts come to mind to disregard them, going back to the mantra." The suggested sequence of meditation: Twice a day in the morning before breakfast and in the evening before dinner, for 20 minutes at a time. Meditation techniques are usually done in a quiet room, lying down, and with eyes closed. The mode of behavior is passive —just let it happen.

Benson observed physiological changes during meditation that were somewhat different from those occurring during sleep. He labeled that group of changes the "Relaxation Response." In his research, he found that during meditation there was a decrease in oxygen consumption, respiratory rate, heart rate, and blood pressure. Significantly different from sleep was the increase in alpha-waves. Alpha-waves are a measure of one form of brain activity that increases when someone is sitting quietly with their eyes closed. Individuals report feeling fully relaxed when alpha waves are increased. It is interesting to note that a small percentage of the population has great difficulty producing alpha-waves; they are unable to enter a relaxed state. If an individual in a relaxed state is asked to perform a cognitive task—to spell a word, for example—the alpha-waves are reduced or disappear.

Benson and others found that a variety of techniques elicited the physiological changes of the Relaxation Response: self-hypnosis, progressive relaxation, autogenic training, Sentic cycles, zen, and yoga.

The progressive relaxation technique, developed as early as 1938 by Edmond Jacobson, is used to treat anxiety. The patient learns relaxation by tensing and relaxing the major muscle groups and focusing on the difference in bodily feelings when muscles are tensed and relaxed. In that way, he can identify which parts of the body are tense so that he can focus on a fuller state of relaxation.

In autogenic training, developed by Johannes Schultz and Wolfgang Luthe in 1959, the patient uses her imagination to develop relaxed levels of feeling in the body. In the first exercise, the patient focuses on feelings of heaviness in the limbs; in the next exercise, she focuses on feelings of warmth. The patient's imagination is used to produce the way the body feels when it is relaxed.

In Sentic cycles, developed by Manfred Clynes, the imagination is used to induce eight psychological states—emotionlessness, anger, hate, grief, sexuality, joy, love, and reverence. The physiological changes that occur during each state are highly predictable.

Sentic states are another doorway into a place where we can communicate and invoke our inner power.

If your preferred entry into the inner room is via relaxation, meditation, zen, or yoga, or any other approach which puts you in touch with your body and mind, you can still use the exercises and visualizations of self-hypnosis to communicate with your inner self. Relax, breathe, listen, and let yourself explore ways to grow and change.

BIOFEEDBACK

Prior to the late 1960s, physiologists, as well as physicians, believed that because the body's internal functions were carried out by the autonomic nervous system and reflexes, they were beyond the control of any individual. Though the medical fraternity listened politely to tales from India and the Far East, it was always with a raised eyebrow. Yet, as physiologist Barbara B. Brown points out in her book *Stress and The Art of Biofeedback*, "literally, all science had to do to challenge that belief was to look in the mirror. And wink. Winking is learned biofeedback . . . Blinking is . . . a reflex performed automatically a thousand times a day . . . Yet we can also learn to control that reflex. Most people learn how to wink as youngsters, either by working with a mirror or with Mother." As people look in the mirror while trying to blink, the mirror provides them with biofeedback—information that tells them when their body's reactions are getting closer or further away from the goal. Somehow—perhaps from the physician within—that information is merged with the information coming from the muscles in the eyelid and, as a result, people learn to wink.

By placing sensors (devices that can monitor the body's internal activities) at strategic locations on the body, we can record changes in internal activities such as heart rate, blood pressure, temperature, muscle tension, and brain waves—very much in the same way we take a person's pulse. We can then electronically make that information available to the individual. In a sense, we create an electronic mirror through which the individual can observe the changes.

For example, during an acute attack of Raynaud's Syndrome—a disease that affects the blood flow in a patient's extremities—a patient's hands or feet become cold, blue, and extremely painful. The blood vessels are severely constricted. In biofeedback therapy, a sensor that measures temperature—a thermistor—is attached to a patient's hand, and the changes in temperature are projected electronically on a screen. The patient then imagines that his hand is getting warmer as he watches the temperature screen for feedback. In clinical practice, patients have often learned to increase the temperature in their hands and feet as much as 10 degrees.

Barbara Brown succinctly describes the best way to use this particular doorway into our inner selves: "Apparently the trick in biofeedback is to get the consciousness out of the picture, let the information pour in, and let whatever mental giant resides in the great unconscious use that information to put our body's activities aright."

EXERCISE

There are a number of important health benefits associated with regular programs of exercise. It is now commonly known that moderate exercise and a low-fat diet, are key factors in reducing the risk and severity of heart attacks. Exercise, in and of itself, has been associated with positive changes in cholesterol levels and is part of any weight reduction program. It has consistently produced improvement in body condition and served to maintain weight loss in obese individuals.

However, the benefits of exercise extend beyond the physical. Researchers report that a number of permanent psychological changes are fostered by a regular program of exercise. One of the most universally accepted changes is the "feeling good" sensation that accompanies any repeated physical activity, even such a relatively low-impact activity as walking. The psychological effects of *vigorous* exercise, however, are more pronounced. Running, for example, has been shown to be as effective as psychotherapy in reducing depression. And in a 1972 study reported in the *American Journal of Physical Medicine*, vigorous exercise was shown to be superior to a well-known tranquilizer in reducing tension.

Of particular interest is the phenomenon known as the "runner's high." In this state, the runner is internally focused and in full contact with a sense of self. I believe that this "high" feeling signals the entry into the inner room and an increase in receptivity—an ideal state in which to use suggestive, self-hypnotic exercises.

Kenneth E. Callen, a physician, has written in the

American Journal of Clinical Hypnosis that "in recent years it has become commonplace to read in popular running magazines of unusual mental phenomena occurring with running. Some of the descriptions bear a strong resemblance to hypnotic states . . . with wide variation in depth, increased receptivity to internal events, absorption and vivid imagery."

SYSTEMATIC DESENSITIZATION

Almost completely removed from the slow process of analysis and the intricate motives that drive us from infancy on, is the work of Joseph Wolpe and his technique called Systematic Desensitization. Promoting behavioral conditioning above all, Wolpe believes that anxiety "is based on learning at a subcortical level of neural integration, which is not likely to be undone merely because thinking—a cortical affair—has changed." In his view, analytic therapy is beside the point. Used for the treatment of phobias, Systematic Desensitization counteracts overt anxiety. The patient grades a series of dangers from those on the low side of the scale that he can deal with, to those far too stressful and dangerous for him to cope with behaviorally. He then proceeds from lesser forms of danger up to the greater ones, finally reaching the target symptom. Given a severe case of agoraphobia, for example, a Systematic Desensitization patient might begin by opening one window in her living room, then two windows in her bedroom, then spending a few minutes each day in the vestibule of her apartment building, then walking down to the corner and back, then around the block, and so on, thus paring away the phobia a little at a time.

Does a system built so radically upon conditioning work? For some, it appears so (Wolpe claims that his "therapy improves or cures nine out of ten patients who give it a real chance, compared with maybe six out of ten for psychoanalysis.").

DRUG USE

It has been nearly 40 years since the first psychotropic drugs were introduced into psychiatric practice in the U.S., and the results of spiraling drug consumption have been both good and bad. I would be remiss if I did not clarify my position on the use of psychotropic drugs. When I find my patients either unable to function or self-destructive, I refer them to a psychiatrist whose specialty is psychopharmacology—an expert in the use of psychotropic medication. While he monitors medication, I continue with psychotherapy. Research has shown that when drugs are used knowledgeably, judiciously, and in conjunction with psychotherapy, they are more effective than either drugs or psychotherapy alone. For example, the drug chlorpromazine has made it possible for severely troubled mental patients to live at home and hold jobs rather than rust away in a hospital. Clomipramine has been found to be effective in reducing the urge to commit obsessive acts in patients with an obsessive-compulsive disorder. Other, milder drugs, used judiciously by nonpsychotic patients, have reduced stress and panic and have proven to be a particular help at certain stages in therapy by opening the patient more completely. These are positive results of drug use. Used as an adjunct to therapy and administered to patients who simply cannot function without them because of profound depression or psychosis, drugs play a vital and positive role in treatment.

Since psychotropic drugs were introduced, however, they have also been vastly overused and often misused. It has been widely documented that Americans have come to depend on drugs for everything from sleeping at night to waking up in the morning, from dieting to facing the boss, and from getting on an airplane to having sex. We have learned (and are still learning) the hard way that drugs are rarely a solution to anything, and they sometimes mask our real problems and authentic feelings. It is a mistake to take a tranquilizer in order to reduce anxiety when anxiety —let's say in preparing for an important business meeting—may be the appropriate response. It is dangerous to use drugs to make yourself feel safe when, in reality, you are at risk. It is unwise to take drugs to make yourself feel happy when grief is called for. It is folly to take drugs to pump yourself full of energy when your body is fatigued almost to the point of collapse. Drugs used to mask the truth of mind and body represent a serious form of abuse. Eventually, your body and mind will rebel. You're more likely to deal with problems effectively when you realize how disturbed you are by them instead of masking them with pills. This is true both of external problems—dealing with an irascible boss or an irate in-law—and internal ones. If you are suffering from free-floating anxiety, don't look for a solution in a bottle of pills. You need to see a therapist, who will assist you in working through problems. If taking drugs keeps you from turning to therapy in the first place, they are doing you harm.

In the final chapter of this book, we will examine ways in which you can tap your inner power by yourself, with the help of a friend, or when necessary, with the help of a professional. By learning to create an experience tailored to your own specific needs, you will begin to have clear access to a power you already possess.

Chapter 8

DEVELOPING YOUR OWN
SELF-HYPNOSIS EXERCISE

EACH OF you is about to begin a journey into a complex
and mysterious world—yourself. For some, the journey may be difficult. For all of you, it will take time.
Once you learn the self-hypnosis technique, you will
be able to develop the ability, over time, to realisti-
cally modify your reactions and behavior. As you
begin to utilize the power to change your behavior,
emotional changes will also take place; you will begin
to feel growing within you a sense of empowerment
and pride.

You may want to seek out a qualified professional
to "teach" you the method, or you may want to learn
it from books or tapes. What I hope I've imparted to
you are the many reasons to want to learn how to
create your own exercises, so that the practice of self-
hypnosis can become a regular part of your everyday
life. You may be facing a problem or situation that
demands immediate attention. You may want to break
a habit, or connect with your inner self through the
use of self-hypnosis. Or you may already be using an

exercise that doesn't quite work and would like to know how to make it more effective. Or your problem may be similar to one you've read about in this or another book and you would like to create an exercise to suit yourself. Or you may simply be curious and want to learn about, and test out, this form of self-empowerment.

EVALUATING YOUR HYPNOTIC CAPACITY

Only a small percentage of people (5 to 15 percent) will have the hypnotic capacity sought by the stage hypnotist when he is looking for volunteers for his nightclub act. Most of you will be in the mid-range (65 percent of the population). Only those on the very upper end of the HIP scale are capable of complete age regression; only they can totally reexperience events as if they were actually happening. Therapeutically, however, they are not necessarily more successful than those with a lesser capacity. Where you are on the scale tells you more about how your self-hypnotic experience will *feel* than how effective it can be.

Some sense of your hypnotic capacity can be drawn from the way you respond to a series of familiar situations. On the 10-question test that follows, score yourself on a scale of 0–3, where 0 is never, 1 seldom, 2 occasionally, and 3 often or always.

Question   *Score 0–3*

1. Do you ever become so involved in a television program, movie, or play that you lose awareness of where you are?   _____

2. In the midst of a conversation, has the person you are talking to suddenly asked "Where have you gone?" _____

3. When reading or hearing about somebody else's experiences, do you get deeply involved? _____

4. Have you ever waited at a red light and suddenly realized that the person in the car behind you has been honking his horn because the light has changed? _____

5. Have you ever been able to recall an experience so vividly that you almost felt you were actually reliving it? _____

6. Have you ever been deeply moved by an eloquent or poetic speaker? _____

7. Have you ever arrived home with an object that a salesperson convinced you was perfectly suited to you only to realize that you really didn't want it? _____

8. Did you ever glance at the clock while engrossed in a book to find that it's an hour later than you thought? _____

9. Do people complain they've told you about important things which you cannot remember? _____

10. Have you ever been physically hurt and only realized it later when you found a cut or a bruise? _____

If your score is between 20 and 30, you probably have a high hypnotic capacity. Scores from 10 to 19 indicate mid-range potential. If you scored less than 10, you are likely to be at the lower-end of the hypnotic scale but, even so, if you answered *any* question with a two or a three, your potential is greater than your overall score suggests.

Another indication of your hypnotic capacity—

and probably the quickest predictor—can be drawn from the HIP eyeroll, which is one part of the HIP evaluation (described in Chapter 3). The eyeroll test can be done with the help of an associate—ideally, an interested friend. You proceed by sitting and facing your friend, asking him to draw an imaginary line across the corners of your eyes. Then, without moving your head, you look up as if you're trying to see your eyebrows. As you continue to look up, close your eyes slowly. As your eyelids approach the imaginary line, ask your friend to tell you what proportion of your pupil can be seen and whether you squinted as your eyes closed.

Score a four if your pupil is totally hidden as the lid approaches the imaginary line. If your friend can see a quarter of the pupil, score a three. If he can see a half, score a two; for three quarters, a one; and score a zero if all of the pupil shows. A score of four is the highest; zero the lowest. If your friend told you that you squinted, add one point to your score for a slight squint, and three points if it was extreme. The highest combined score for the eye-roll and squint is a four, which is the highest level of hypnotic capacity that can be measured by this test. (A score of five is possible, but only with additional testing, after a complete HIP examination.)

For a more precise and accurate idea of your capacity, a professional test (such as the complete HIP, the Stanford Scale, or Harvard Group test among others) would need to be administered by a psychologist. Until then, you can use the results of the quiz and the HIP eyeroll procedure as an indicator. Keep in mind that regardless of your level of hypnotic capacity, almost everybody can benefit from the technique—as we learned from Marcus, the surgery patient who was

ROLL

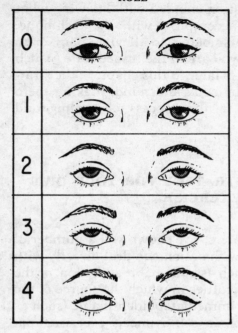

SQUINT

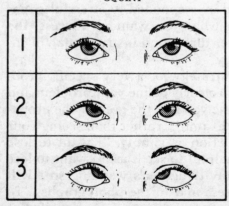

Eye-Roll Test
for Hypnotizability.

Prepared by:
Herbert Spiegel, M.D.
PM 4 & 5 Courses
College of Physicians & Surgeons
Columbia University.

at the extreme low-end of the scale. The most important factor is motivation coupled with knowing what it is you want to accomplish with the technique, whether it is to stop smoking, to alleviate pain, or to take an exam. Once you are in the trance state (which you will learn to enter later in this chapter), the strategy is to talk to your body and mind, making them active participants in the process of healing and change.

CREATING THE STRATEGY FOR YOUR OWN SELF-HYPNOSIS EXERCISE

In the previous chapters, I've shown you a number of strategies I created with patients to deal directly with specific problems, such as pain, habit addiction, or the discomforts and difficulties in which the source of the problem was not so immediately identifiable (such as impotence or anger). In self-hypnosis exercises, patients used their imagination and memory to change the way they reacted or responded to stressful situations. Depending on what you want to address, the exercises can be either direct and instructional, or indirect and exploratory.

As you create a strategy for a very specific problem, it is important to clearly define your problem and goal. The more specific you are, the greater the probability of success. For example, rather than seeing your goal for weight reduction as simply: "I want to lose weight," it is more helpful to see it as: "I want to lose weight in time for my daughter's wedding so I will look better in my dress and in the photographs." To help you create the proper strategy for yourself, I've outlined these three steps for you, followed by a number of examples.

1. **Identify the problem and the changes you would like to see.** Say to yourself or write down: "This is what I do that bothers me, and this is what I wish were different. This is how I would like to change." Because motivation is critical, ask yourself: How important is it for me to change? How committed am I?

   (To help smokers with these questions, a special *Smokers Self-testing Kit* was developed by Daniel Horn, Ph.D. through the Public Health Service and is available through the U.S. Government Printing Office.)

2. **Identify the benefits.** Describe to yourself the ways in which you would benefit by dealing with your problem and changing the situation. List as many benefits as you can think of.

3. **Imagine yourself problem-free.** If you can, try to remember a time when you were free of the problem. How did it feel? How did you act? If you've never been without the problem, imagine what it would be like to be free of it. How would you feel? How would you act? To help you create the proper images for your exercise, sit down, close your eyes, and make yourself comfortable. Then imagine yourself behaving the way you want to behave, acting the way you want to act. Draw from memory and your imagination, using all of your senses. Imagine both changes and benefits. Vary colors, odors, and sounds. Change, modify, and play with the images until they feel right for you.

EXAMPLE A: Cynthia

My problem:

I get tense and anxious when I find myself in crowded places. I would like to go when and where I want to and feel relaxed.

The benefits if I change:
- I'll be able to go to the theater with my friends.
- I'll have a wider range of jobs I can pursue.
- I'll be able to go with my kids to their school events.

The ways I would like to act and feel:
- I picture myself as I was at my son's fifth birthday when we went as a family to Disneyland. I felt free and easy and in love with everyone and everything, even in the midst of large crowds.
- I picture myself going to a Saturday matineé with my three best friends, Nancy, Marcie, and Sheryl.
- I picture myself going to a wonderful job in the newest downtown office skyscraper.

EXAMPLE B: Judy

My problem:

I'm 20 pounds overweight and I want so much to be slimmer for my daughter's wedding.

The benefits if I change:
- I'll look better at my daughter's wedding.
- I'll photograph better for the wedding album.
- I'll feel better about myself.
- I'll be more attractive to others.

The ways I would like to act and feel:

I picture myself as I felt sometime ago when I went to a wonderful French restaurant and chose from the menu carefully, ordering exactly what I wanted. I ate very little and very slowly, but savored every bite of food. I remember a friend once telling me how sensual it was watching a slim, Parisian woman eat dessert. How she ate little spoonfuls, savoring each mouthful. That's the way I ate, savoring and tasting the food. I was surprised to find myself satisfied after eating only a small amount. I imagine myself carefully choosing my food, going out of my way to eat what I really want; I see myself doing the same thing at every meal. I take my time; I savor and enjoy the food. I see myself at my daughter's wedding looking slim and attractive, enjoying her wedding and loving the way I look and feel.

EXAMPLE C: David

My problem:
I want to stop smoking.

The benefits if I change:
- I'll feel better.
- I won't always be short of wind and I can go back to playing basketball.
- I won't be ostracized at work.
- I'll set a good example for my daughter—I don't want her to smoke.

The ways I would like to act and feel:
I picture myself seeing a friend who still smokes; he is ashen-faced, gasping for breath, cigarette in hand. He is no longer able to play basketball; it is a thing of the past. Then I picture myself choosing not to smoke whenever I get the urge. I realize I'm giving myself the gift of life. I'm playing basketball! I can walk into a meeting without looking

around for an ashtray; everyone is pleased that I've given up smoking. I see my daughter refusing her friend's offer of a cigarette. She's saying to my friend: "No one in my family smokes! My father used to, but he got smart."

EXAMPLE D: Jennifer

My problem:

I'm afraid to go to the dentist although I know I need to go.

The benefits if I change:
- My gums will stop bleeding.
- I'll get rid of the ache in the back of my mouth.
- I'll have fewer problems with my teeth as I grow older.

The ways I would like to act and feel:
- I picture myself talking to my friends about finding a dentist I can trust, and although I feel anxious, I set up an appointment.
- I picture myself on the way to the office feeling very pleased that I'm taking care of myself. I enter the office, still a little anxious, but let my body relax while I'm telling the dentist about my problems. As he begins to examine my teeth, I focus on my body being relaxed and limp. I sense that the dentist is competent and cares about taking good care of me. I can see myself at the end of treatment with healthy pink gums and white teeth. I'm pleased that I've taken steps to deal with the problem.

EXAMPLE E: Larry

My problem:

I want to rid myself of anxiety when I speak up in front of people.

The benefits if I change:
- · I will be able to go to professional meetings and feel comfortable publicly expressing my point of view.
- · I can become active in the local little league, and not be afraid of winning an award or having to give a speech.

The ways I would like to act and feel:
- · I picture myself attending a local meeting of my professional society: I stand at the microphone intelligently commenting on a proposal. After the discussion, various colleagues come over to talk about my comments. I am very pleased.
- · My son and I are on our way to a little league game. It's the first time that I have volunteered to help with the coaching. He is very proud and excited.

Once you have gone through the steps yourself and know what you want to accomplish in self-hypnosis, you will be able to use these images while in the trance state to let your body and mind know the way you want to behave, act, and feel. You can then "prescribe" the exercises for yourself two or three times a day for at least 90 seconds each time, until you have accomplished your goal. In summary, here are the basic instructions for creating the visualizations or images you may want to project during your self-hypnosis exercise:

1. Start by using your imagination to create an exercise that contains examples of the way you would like to feel and act. The exercise will be most effective if it is based on times or situa-

tions in which you felt and acted the way you would like to feel and act.

2. Include as part of the exercise the benefits you would derive when your behavior changes. Envision the change in behavior as a gift you are giving yourself.

3. See yourself behaving in ways you want others to see you, as well as in ways you want to see yourself. Most of us want to be seen in a favorable light that will make us proud of ourselves.

4. Create the exercise so that it says: "This is the way I want to act, feel, and be seen. This is what I dislike about the way I am now and would like to change." Be sure to frame things with a positive emphasis. Avoid the shoulds and should nots; we tend to use them to diminish ourselves.

5. Modify your exercise when it begins to feel superficial. Patients have told me that they need to change the images after a month or so in order for the exercise to remain effective.

Patients often ask: "How do I show myself examples of how to act and feel? Do I talk to myself and tell myself what to do? Do I just see or feel myself acting the way I want to, the way I do in a dream? Can I just feel the way I want myself to feel and act? Can I imagine it happening as if I'm in a play or a movie?" My answer is that you can use any or all of those techniques. Use every dimension of your imagination to communicate your message.

There are some problems for which an imaginary movie or TV screen is the most effective way to project visualizations. For example, you can use a three-paneled screen—a multipart image—to help you sort out and understand your present situation, conflicts, and goals for change. The screen serves as a framework for reflecting on your experience. Here are the steps:

1. Once you are in the trance state, you begin by imagining a screen with three sections, or panels. Onto the center panel, project something that occurred that day. It could be a meeting with your boss; last night's date; a scene from a movie or a play that touched you; or the last step in solving a vexing problem. Let one event flow into the next, without direction. What you project can be real or imaginary, past or future, but is particularly effective when recollections stir up strong feelings. Fill the scenes with as much detail as possible and let yourself freely play out your role in them. Whatever is disturbing you will likely show up in these recollections.

2. As your experiences play out on the center screen, identify those things that make you anxious, or angry, or sad, or frightened, or frustrated. These are the aspects of your experience that you can now project onto the screen's left-hand panel.

3. Next, identify those things that make you feel warm inside or creative, excited, involved. Project those experiences onto the screen's right-hand panel.

4. Once scenes are playing out on the center, left- and right-hand panels, sit back comfortably and relax. Observe and reflect on the contents

of the three screens. See what thoughts, feelings, and ideas come to mind. Whenever you feel ready, start the steps to bring yourself out of trance.

Eileen, the musician who thought she could no longer compose, saw herself in the center screen interacting with her parents, telling them about her work, and listening to their reactions. Her reflections made her aware of how much she was doing to please her parents and not herself; she came to understand that her work blockage had been an unconscious protest of a situation she hadn't been aware of. She moved the blocked images of herself to the left-hand screen and, on the right, imagined herself composing for her own pleasure and sense of accomplishment—without her parents in the picture.

There is another way that we make use of the screen idea when we are in trance. You may recall that in some of the exercises I helped create for patients, the screens were split in half. For example, in Martha's exercise for losing weight, the left half of the screen showed her at her present weight, and the right half showed the way she wanted to look and feel in three months. Another weight-control patient told me she saw herself in the left-hand panel in tight-fitting pants that she could not zip up and, in the right-hand panel, she saw herself standing on a scale that showed her at the weight she wanted to be. A split screen shows where you are now and where, ideally, you will be.

You can also utilize a single-screen approach, enabling you to see yourself acting and feeling the way you want to be. For example, if you are using the exercise to stop smoking, you can see yourself at a party, and someone comes up to you offering you a cigarette and you see yourself saying, "No, thank you, I no longer smoke."

The above examples apply mainly to exploring your feelings, and letting your body know the way you want it to act and feel. Self-hypnosis exercises are also effectively used for dealing with pain. Three of the more common approaches are as follows:

1. Glove Anesthesia: After entering the trance state, open your eyes slowly and stare at your hand. Imagine there is a spot on the palm that feels as if someone had injected novocaine. Let the feeling of numbness begins to spread, just as it does when you're at the dentist. Feel the gentle, tingling numbness entering your fingers and your hand. When the feeling covers your hand like a glove, place your hand where you feel the pain. Track the numbness as it moves from your hand to the source of the pain. Slowly, the pain will begin to leave. Feel the spread of tingling numbness.

2. Redirection of Attention: In the trance state, as you start to feel discomfort, transport yourself to an unusual and special place where it is warm and the sun is shining. The light brings out the colors of your surroundings. As you listen, you are caressed by bird songs and the wind. You feel very much at peace.

3. Changing Size and Location: While in trance, focus on the pain; study it carefully so you can tell exactly where it is. Now, imagine that the pain is inside a hollow ball of clay. As you warm the clay with your hands, it becomes more malleable and you can slowly squeeze the ball, making it smaller and smaller. As the ball

shrinks, the pain itself grows smaller and smaller and finally disappears.

ENTERING THE TRANCE STATE

When trying something new—such as learning to enter trance—there is a tendency to split ourselves into two parts: the part that participates in the experience and the other that critically evaluates and observes. For many different learning experiences, this is a good way to begin. The most effective way to learn to enter trance, however, is neither to observe nor evaluate, but to be as relaxed as possible and totally flow along with the experience.

When you are ready to begin, find a quiet, comfortable place where you will not be disturbed. Schedule enough time so that you can practice going in and out of trance at least three or four times. Assume that in the beginning it will take time for you to become proficient. Be aware of the variability of trance experience. The depth of involvement can vary from time to time. Give yourself time to experiment.

If you decide to use the two-person technique for entering trance, find a friend you trust who has an easy disposition. Have that friend slowly read you the directions for entering trance. If you prefer to work alone, you can record a hypnotic induction on audio- or videotape and play it back for yourself, or you can memorize the directions, using your inner voice to talk yourself through the steps. You can use one of the three trance-induction procedures given below, or choose any other from the books in the list of references. The important thing is to find one that works best for you.

THE HIP SELF-HYPNOSIS INDUCTION

1. Sitting or lying down, make yourself as comfortable as you can.
2. With your head in a relaxed position, look up—only with your eyes—as if you are trying to see your eyebrows.
3. Close your eyes, but keep looking up.
4. Take a deep breath, and hold your breath for the count of three—one . . . two . . . three.
5. Let go. Let your breath out, let your eyes relax, and let your body float.
6. Imagine yourself floating down, as if you were on a soft feathery couch or cloud, letting yourself enter your safe, comfortable place.
   (At this point, you want to be totally relaxed and inwardly focused, ready to use whatever strategy you've created to deal with your problem or situation. You are ready to talk with your body and mind.)
7. Invoke the imagery you've created. Stay with these images for 90 seconds, or more if you like.
8. To bring yourself out of trance in a relaxed, comfortable way, count backwards slowly from three to one. At three—get ready; at two—look up; at one—open your eyes and slowly permit them to come into focus.

THE REVERSE HAND-LEVITATION INDUCTION

1. Sitting in a comfortable armchair, place your elbow on the armrest. Choose whatever arm you prefer.

2. Bend your elbow and lift your hand to an upright position.

3. Now, study your hand as if it belonged to another person. Focus your eyes on a single part of the hand. Study that part as if you were a sculptor, artist, or a physician and wanted to be able to duplicate the hand in your mind's eye.

4. Notice the details that appear as you study the hand. Notice the colors, shadows, and the texture; notice how they change.

5. You might find that the hand begins to feel heavier or lighter (it makes no difference) and begins to move. When it moves, let it move very, very slowly. Let it move less than an inch, every five minutes.

6. As you study the hand, your eyes may begin to blink. You can let them do so, or keep your eyes open if you so choose.

7. If you choose to let your eyes close and your hand float, keep the image of your hand in your mind's eye and float to your own safe, comfortable place.

(At this point, you want to be totally relaxed and inwardly focused, ready to use whatever strategy you've created to deal with your problem or situation. You are ready to talk with your body and mind.)

8. Invoke the imagery you've created. Stay with these images for 90 seconds, or more if you like.

9. To bring yourself out of trance in a relaxed, comfortable manner, count slowly backwards from 10 to one. 10 . . . 9 . . . 8 . . . 7 . . . 6 . . . 5

...4...3...2...1. When you reach three, let your eyes slowly begin to open, and then fully open at the count of one.

THE KRESKIN AUTO-CONDITIONING INDUCTION

Kreskin, who uses the term "auto-suggestion" rather than self-hypnosis, proposes another way to make yourself receptive to suggestion. He calls it auto-conditioning—that is, a series of mental relaxation exercises patterned somewhat as follows: First, after getting yourself in a passive frame of mind, you mentally melt and give your imagination free rein. Then, follow these steps in sequence:

1. Sitting in deep chair or lying down, make yourself comfortable.
2. Reflect for a few seconds on a time and place that left you deeply relaxed—a quiet afternoon on the beach, falling asleep in front of a fireplace after a walk in the snow, lying in deep shade on a riverbank. Recall as vividly as you can the total experience.
3. Close your eyes and think of a soft, mellow color like blue or green, or the pink hues of roses.
4. After a few seconds, take three deep breaths; hold the third and the deepest and mentally repeat the color image three times.
5. Exhale and let your entire body go limp. Make no effort to move a muscle. Simply stay relaxed and count backwards, mentally, from 50 to zero—very slowly.
(When you reach zero, you want to be totally

relaxed and inwardly focused, ready to use whatever strategy you've created to deal with your problem or situation. You are ready to talk with your body and mind.)

6. Invoke the imagery you've created. Stay with these images for 90 seconds, or longer if you like.

7. Then, when you are ready to bring yourself out, count forward from one to three. Then, open your eyes.

If you already use meditation, the relaxation response, yoga, or other techniques, feel free to enter your inner room through those doorways. If you need help in learning how to induce trance, you may want to seek help from a professional.

When I work with a patient, I try to create an exercise that is achievable. Motivation and understanding are keys to success—a combination that should be your goal when you create your own self-hypnosis exercise.

In providing you with a step-by-step procedure, I don't mean to minimize the difficulty involved in creating effective exercises. When you are dealing with emotionally charged issues, at first it may be hard for you to see positive ways to change your behavior. After all, you may have been struggling with a particular issue for many years. You may have to acknowledge that some issues are so complex that, by yourself, you may not be able to find effective strategies for dealing with them. Perhaps in such cases the help of a psychologist or psychiatrist is needed.

Long ago I learned that there is no universal cure. There is no magic wand you and I can wave to change what troubles us. What you have is the power within you. With that power you can change your beliefs, your behavior, your responses, and your previously uncontrolled, automatic reactions. If you can truly accept the things you cannot control—not just the weather or the color of your eyes, but other people's behavior—you can focus more clearly on what is the most possible to control: yourself. The movie *Star Wars* provides a striking example of the uses of personal power. We see the hero trying to raise his space craft from a swamp. The guru he's working with helps him to understand that in order to use the power, he must accept the fact that he has it. That's precisely what I have proposed in this book—rather than trusting my belief in you, begin to act as if *you* have the power. In *Star Wars* the hero raises the space craft from the swamp by using his own inner power. He accomplishes something that's important to him by evoking the capacity that, if we only come to know it, resides in us all. The power to change belongs to you.

CHAPTER NOTES

Chapter 1

Through personal instruction, observation, and books like: O. McGill, *Encyclopedia of Stage Hypnotism* (Colon, Michigan: Abbot's Magic Novelty Company, 1947); Harry Arons, *Techniques of Speed Hypnosis* (Newark, NJ: Power Publishers, 1953). Arons writes that: "The stage hypnotist always selects the *best* of the 'volunteers' for the first instantaneous hypnosis, as his success or failure with the first subject largely determines the course of the rest of the demonstration."

In a study of the self-regulation of physiological processes: Jonathan Cohen and Keith Sedlacek, "Attention and Autonomic Self-regulation," *Psychosomatic Medicine* 45, 1983: 243–257.

Today, several national, professional societies of hypnosis:
Society for Clinical and Experimental Hypnosis
129-A King Park Drive
Liverpool, NY 13090
315 652-7299

American Society of Clinical Hypnosis
2250 East Devon Avenue, Suite 336
Des Plaines, IL 60018
312 297-3317

Division 30—Psychological Hypnosis
American Psychological Association
1200 Seventeenth Street, NW
Washington, DC 20036

As Lewis Alexander defined it: Louis Alexander, "Hypnotically Induced Hallucinations," *American Journal of Clinical Hypnosis* 15, 1972: 6.

When demonstrating the hypnotic state at work: Louis J. West, "Physiological Theories of Hypnosis." In *The Nature of Hypnosis,* edited by Milton V. Kline. New York: Postgraduate Center for Psychotherapy and The Institute for Research in Hypnosis, 1962.

Psychiatrist Milton Erickson argues: Milton H. Erickson, "Hypnotic Psychotherapy." In *The Collected Papers of Milton H. Erickson on Hypnosis.* Vol. 4, *Innovative Hypnotherapy,* edited by Ernest L. Rossi. New York: Irvington, 1980.

In an interview conducted with Dr. Albert Schweitzer: Norman Cousins, *Anatomy of an Illness as Perceived by the Patient* (New York: W. W. Norton, 1979).

Chapter 2

I was particularly struck by an article: William Gruen, "A Successful Application of Systematic Self-relaxation and Self-suggestion about Postoperative Reactions in a Case of Cardiac Surgery," *International J of Clinical and Experimental Hypnosis* 20, 1972: 145–151.

. . . an article about preoperative hospital procedures: M. A. Farber, *New York Times,* 1978. Story on the poisonous drug Curaree, and the way in which it is used during surgery.

Hans Selye identifies three stages of the body's reaction to stress: Hans Selye, *The Stress of Life* (New York: McGraw-Hill, 1956); Hans Selye, *Stress Without Distress* (New York: Signet, 1974).

Three doctors at UCLA Medical School: Emil G. Bishay, Grant Stevens and Chingmuh Lee, "Hypnotic Control of Upper Gastrointestinal Hemorrhage: A Case Report, *American J of Clinical Hypnosis* 27, 1984: 22–25.

. . . reactions are not totally interrupted by general anesthesia: David B. Cheek, "Awareness of Meaningful Sounds Under General Anesthesia: Considerations and a Review of the Literature 1959–1979." In *Theoretical and Clinical Aspects of Hypnosis*, edited by Harold J. Wain. Miami, Florida: Symposia Specialists: Obstetrics and Gynecology, 1981.

. . . and preoperative hypnotic suggestion can play a vital role: Bennett reported that suggestions given to patients undergoing orthopedic surgery of the spine reduced blood loss during surgery from 800cc to 350cc; Henry L. Bennett, "Preop Suggestions Reduce Blood Loss," *Human Aspects of Anesthesia*, January/February, 1985.

There is also evidence that patients under general anesthesia can hear: Harry L. Bennett, Hamilton S. Davis, and Jefferey A. Giannini, "Non-verbal Response to Intrasoperative Conversation," *British Journal of Anaesthesiology* 57, 1985: 174–179.

. . . told that their postoperative period of convalescence would be shortened: R. E. Pearson, "Response to Suggestions Given Under General Anesthesia," *American J of Clinical Hypnosis*, 4, 1961: 106–114.

. . . used hypnotic techniques with 254 of his surgical cases: Fred T. Koulouch, "Role of Suggestion in Surgical convalescence," *Archives of Surgery* 85, 1962: 304–315; Fred T. Koulouch, "Hypnosis and Surgical Convalescence: A Study of Subjective Factors in Postoperative Recovery," *Am J of Clinical Hypnosis*, 7, 1964: 120–129.

Esdaile wrote a report on his work: James Esdaile, *Mesmerism in India and Its Practical Application in Surgery and Medicine* (Hartford, England: Silus Andrus & Son, 1850). Retitled and republished as *Hypnosis in Medicine and Surgery*. An introduction and supplemental reports on hypoanesthesia by William Kroger (New York: Julian Press, 1957).

An 1890 article in the Journal: M. H. Lackersteen, M.D., M.R.C.P., etc., "The Scientific Aspects of Medical Hypnotism, or Treatment by Suggestion," *Journal of the American Medical Association* 15, 1890; 747–751; reprinted *JAMA* 264 (20), November 28, 1990.

.... **hypoanesthesia for the surgical removal of a large tumor:** Don M. Morris, MD; Ronald G. Nathan, PhD; Ronald A. Goebel, PhD and Norman H. Blass, MD, "Hypoanesthesia in the Morbidly Obese," JAMA 252, 1985: 3292–3294.

A cholecystectomy . . . in which self-hypnosis was the sole anesthesia: Victor Rausch, "Cholecystecomy with Self-hypnosis," *Am J Clinical Hypnosis* 22, 1980: 124–199.

. . . **in this country alone there are 300,000 bypass surgeries:** Source: National Center for Health Statistics, *National Hospital Discharge Surgery*, 1989.

. . . **the trance state is biologically essential:** Stephen G. Gilligan, *Therapeutic Trances: Cooperative Principles in Eriksonian Psychotherapy* (New York: Brunner-Mazel, 1987).

. . . **individual experiences with self-hypnosis:** Erica Fromm, et al., "The Phenomena and Characteristics of Self-hypnosis," *The International J of Experimental and Clinical Hypnosis* 29, 1981: 189–246.

. . . **the Hypnotic Induction Profile (HIP), the clinical evaluation of hypnotic capacity:** Herbert Spiegel and David Spiegel, *Trance & Treatment: Clinical Uses of Hypnosis* (New York: Basic Books, 1978).

. . . **through the natural power of his own trance ability:** Reynolds Price, *Clear Pictures* (New York: Atheneum, 1989).

. . . **internal locus of control:** Julian Rotter, psychologist, quoted in Anthony F. Grasha *Practical Applications of Psychology, Third Edition* (Chicago: Scott Foresman, 1987), 186.

. . . **and to project onto that screen a memory from the past:** Herbert Spiegel and David Spiegel, *Trance & Treatment: Clinical Uses of Hypnosis* (New York: Basic Books, 1978).

... **the need to control is an emotional response:** Nico H. Frijda, "The Laws of Emotion, *American Psychologist* 43, 1988: 349–358.

... **our hidden observer is a function of the ego:** Ernest R. Hilgard, "Divided Consciousness in Hypnosis: The Implications of the Hidden Observer." In *Hypnosis: Developments in Research and New Perspectives, Second Edition,* edited by Erika Fromm & Ronald E. Shor. New York: Aldine Publishing Company, 1979.

... **in a study of the coping skills of dieters:** Carlos M. Grillo, Saul Shiffman and Rena R. Wing, "Relapse Crisis and Coping Among Dieters," *J of Consulting and Clinical Psychology* 57, 1989: 488–495.

... **addictive behavior starts as a form of self-medication:** Edward J. Khantzian, "The Ego, the Self and Opiate Addiction: Theoretical and Treatment Considerations, *International Review of Psycho-Analysis* 5, 1978: 189–198.

Chapter 5

... **that gave the physician within a chance:** Norman Cousins, *Anatomy of an Illness as Perceived by the Patient* (New York: W. W. Norton, 1979).

Chapter 6

... **learning not of specific skills or acts, but of basic attitudes of trust and distrust:** L. Joseph Stone and Joseph Church, *Childhood and Adolescence* (New York: Random House, 1957).

... **the first of a series of critical alternatives:** Erik H. Erickson, *Childhood and Society* (New York: W. W. Norton, 1950).

... **early memories and experiences, a key to emotional life, are stored in visceral rather than cognitive memories:** Joseph LeDoux, "Cognitive-emotional Interactions in the Brain," *Cognition and Emotion* 3, 1989: 267–289.

Therapy results from an inner resynthesis: Milton H. Erickson, "Hypnotic Psychotherapy," in *The Collected Papers of Milton H. Erickson on Hypnosis. Volume IV—Innovative Hypnotherapy*, edited by Ernest L. Rossi. New York: Irvington, 1980.

In real life, Derek Jacobi: Joseph C. Koenenn. "Stage Fright, Yes, Even for Derek Jacobi." *Newsday*, NY Part 2, Sunday, November 8, 1987, 11.

... physical discomfort and thoughts of unpleasant occurrences can activate angry feelings and ideas: Leonard Berkowitz, "On the Formation and Regulation of Anger and Aggression: A Cognitive-neoassociative Analysis," *American Psychologist* 45, 1990: 494–503. This research challenges the wide spread belief—held by both professionals and lay persons—that anger is only aroused "as a result of a perceived threat or the belief that one has been intentionally mistreated." Berkowitz argues that physical discomfort, frustration and thoughts of unpleasant occurrences can also activate angry feelings and ideas.

Chapter 7

He spoke of blending the pure gold of analysis plentifully with the copper of direct suggestion: Sigmund Freud, "Turnings in the Ways of Analysis (1919)." In *Sigmund Freud: Collected Papers*. Vol. 2, edited by E. Jones. New York: Basic Books, 1959.

The eclectic therapist may combine and incorporate techniques drawn from: Albert Ellis, *Reason and Emotion in Psychotherapy* (New York: Lyle Stuart, 1962); Aaron T. Beck, *Cognitive Therapy and the Emotional Disorders* (New York: International University Press, 1967); Habib Davanloo, "Basic Methodology and Technique of Short-term Dynamic Psychotherapy." In *Basic Principles and Techniques in Short-term Dynamic Psychotherapy*, edited by Habib Davanloo. New York: SP Medical & Scientific, 1978; Peter E. Sifneos, "Principles of Technique in Short-Term Anxiety-provoking Psychotherapy." In *Basic Principles and Techniques in Short-term Dynamic Psychotherapy*, edited by

Habib Davanloo. New York: SP Medical & Scientific, 1978; Milton Erickson and Ernest L. Rossi, In *The Collected Papers of Milton H. Erickson on Hypnosis*, edited by Ernest L. Rossi. New York: Irvington, 1980; Ernest L. Rossi, *The Psychobiology of Mind Body Healing* (New York: W. W. Norton, 1986); Herbert Spiegel and David Spiegel, *Trance & Treatment: Clinical Uses of Hypnosis* (New York: Basic Books, 1978).

While searching for behavioral techniques for lowering blood pressure: Herbert Benson, *The Relaxation Response* (New York: William Morrow, 1975); Herbert Benson, Patricia A. Arns, and John W. Hoffman, "The Relaxation Response and Hypnosis," *The International J. of Clinical and Experimental Hypnosis* 29, 1981: 259–270.

Progressive relaxation: Edmund Jacobson. *You Must Relax.* 4th ed. (New York: McGraw Hill, 1962).

Autogenic training: Johannes Schultz and Wolfgang Luthe, *Autogenic Therapy* (New York: Gruen and Stratton, 1969).

Sentic cycles: Manfred Clynes, "Toward a View of Man." In *Biomedical Engineering Systems*, edited by M. Clynes and J. Milsum. New York: McGraw Hill, 1970.

Winking is learned by biofeedback: Barbara B. Brown, *Stress and the Art of Biofeedback* (New York: Harper and Row, 1977.)

. . .the trick in biofeedback is to get the consciousness out of the picture: Barbara B. Brown, *Stress and the Art of Biofeedback* (New York: Harper & Row, 1977).

. . .permanent psychological changes are fostered by a regular program of exercise: William P. Morgan, "Psychological Effects of Exercise," *Behavioral Medicine Update* 4, 1982; 25–29; Wesley E. Sime, "Psychological benefits of exercise," *Advances* 1, 1984: 15–29.

. . . vigorous exercise was shown to be superior to a well-known tranquilizer in reducing tension: H. A. deVries and G. M. Adams, "Electronyographic Comparisons of Single Doses of Exercise and Meprobamate as to Effects on Muscular Relaxation," *American J of Physical Medicine* 51; 1972.

... unusual mental phenomena occurring with running: Kenneth E. Callen, "Auto-hypnosis in Long Distance Runners," *American J Clinical Hypnosis* 26, 1983: 30–36.

Systematic desensitization: Joseph Wolpe, *The Practice of Behavior Therapy* (New York: Permagon Press, 1973).

Chapter 8

The Kreskin auto-conditioning induction: Kreskin (ne George Kresge), *The Amazing World of Kreskin* (New York: Random House, 1973). Well known entertainer and performer, interested in educating public re hypnosis. Billed as "the amazing Kreskin"—does not believe in hypnosis, only suggestion.

FURTHER READINGS

Anisman Hymie, and Robert M. Sacharko. "Stress and Neoplasia: Speculations and Caveats," *Behavioral Medicine Update* 5, 1983; 27–35.

  Research evidence in support of the view that stressful events influence the competence of the immune system. Although the body is initially able to maintain competence for the short haul, without relief the system can fail.

Barbara, Theodore X. "An Alternative Paradigm." In *Hypnosis: Research Developments and Perspectives,* edited by Erika Fromm and Ronald A. Shor. Chicago: Aldine Publishing, 1972.

  An exploration of hypnosis demonstrating the power of suggestion, with or without a formal hypnotic state.

Barbara, Theodore X. "Changing 'unchangeable' Bodily Processes by (Hypnotic) Suggestion: A New Look at Hypnosis, Cognitions, Imagining, and the Mind-Body Problem." In *Imagination and Healing,* edited by Anees A. Sheikh. Farmingdale, New York: Baywood Publishing Company, 1984.

  The author describes and explains how "unchangeable" body structures and processes, for example: the size of a woman's breasts, warts which have existed for many years, and incurable skin diseases can be beneficially altered by suggestion.

Bower, Kenneth S. *Hypnosis for the Seriously Curious* (Monterey, CA: Brooks/Cole Publishing Company, 1976).

  A scientific review of the nature of hypnosis.

  An asterisk (*) indicates that the material contains techniques for entering trance.

Connery, Donald S. *The Inner Source: Exploring Hypnosis with Dr. Herbert Spiegel* (New York: Holt, Rinehart and Winston, 1982).

    Written for the layman, this excellent overview of the therapeutic use of self-hypnosis draws on the case records, classes, and years of experience of the innovative medical doctor who developed the Hypnotic Induction Profile (HIP) and, in Connery's words, "made it possible for medical professionals to make hypnosis part of everyday practice."

Frankel, Fred H. "Significant Developments in Medical Hypnosis during the Past 25 Years," *The International J of Clinical and Experimental Hypnosis* 35, 1987: 231–247.

    Advances in the use of hypnosis in the treatment of medical problems.

Frischolz, Edward J., and David Spiegel. "Hypnosis Is Not Therapy," *Bulletin of the British Society of Experimental and Clinical Hypnosis* 6, 1983: 3–8.

    An analysis of hypnosis as a receptive state for treating illness, showing that, in and of itself, it is not necessarily therapeutic.

Fromm, Erika. "Significant Developments in Clinical Hypnosis during the Past 25 Years," *The International Journal of Clinical and Experimental Hypnosis* 35, 1987: 215–230.

    Advances in the use of hypnosis as a means of alleviating psychological problems.

Fry, William F., and John H. Weakland. "Healing and hypnosis," *Advances* 1, 1984: 60–63.

    Written at a lay level, case studies during which the patient was Fry, a psychiatrist. Fry was successfully treated by Weakland who used hypnotic suggestion to treat Fry's poison oak infection, and at a later date, a case of mumps.

Hammond, D. Corydon, ed. *Hypnotic Suggestions & Metaphors* (New York: W. W. Norton & Co., 1990).

    An official publication of the American Society of Clinical

An asterisk (*) indicates that the material contains techniques for entering trance.

Hypnosis, this book contains over 500 pages of hypnotic and post-hypnotic suggestions which therapists give to their patients in dealing with a variety of medical and psychological problems. Many of the suggestions and images can be adapted for use with self-hypnosis.

* Kroger, William S., and William D. Fezler. *Hypnosis and Behavior Modification: Imagery Conditioning* (Philadelphia: J. B. Lippincott Company, 1976).

Written for professionals, the text contains a variety of structured images (e.g., scenes in a forest, on a beach, in the snow) and describes how to use these scenes therapeutically in hypnosis and self-hypnosis exercises.

Lacey, John I. "Somatic Response Patterning in Stress." *Psychological Stress: Issues in Research*, edited by M. H. Appley and R. Trumbull. New York: Appleton-Century-Crofts, 1967.

Explains why hypnosis and relaxation are effective therapeutic states. The study shows how certain physiological changes, similar to those that are found during hypnosis and relaxation, increase receptivity to suggestion and ideas.

* Pratt, George J., Dennis P. Wood, and Brian M. Alman. *A Clinical Hypnosis Primer* (La Jolla, CA: Psychology and Consulting Associates Press, 1984).

Written for professionals, the text describes hypnotic inductions, and illustrates the use of imagery in self-hypnosis.

Raikov, V. L. "Age Regression to Infancy by Adult Subjects in Deep Hypnosis," *Am J of Clinical Hypnosis* 22, 1980: 156–163.

Research showing that the visceral memories of infancy are accessible during hypnotic age regression.

Reiff, Robert and Martin Scheerer. *Memory and Hypnotic Age Regression* (New York: International Universities Press, 1959).

A comprehensive study which explores the nature and the type of memories that are accessible during hypnotic age regression.

An asterisk (*) indicates that the material contains techniques for entering trance.

* Shames, Richard and Chuck Sterin. *Healing with Mind Power* (Emmaus, PA: Rodale Press, 1978).
    Written for the layman, the book contains more than a dozen examples of self-hypnosis inductions.

Spiegel, David. "The Use of Hypnosis in Controlling Cancer Pain," *Ca-A Cancer Journal for Clinicians* 35, 1985.
    Written for the professional, the article illustrates how to use self-hypnosis to control pain.

An asterisk (*) indicates that the material contains techniques for entering trance.

INDEX

ABOUT THE AUTHORS

STANLEY FISHER, PH.D., a research psychologist with five years of postdoctoral training in psychoanalysis and psychotherapy at New York University, has been in private practice since 1978. He has lectured on medical hypnosis at Columbia University's College of Physicians and Surgeons, and conducted research on self-hypnosis as a preparation for surgery in conjunction with the Albert Einstein College of Medicine. He lives in New York City.

JAMES ELLISON, book editor of *American Health*, is the author of seven critically-acclaimed novels and four nonfiction health and reference books. He lives in New York.